Business Letters for Busy People

Second Edition

More than 130 time-saving, ready-to-use business letters for any occasion

By
Jim Dugger

CAREER PRESS
180 Fifth Avenue
P.O. Box 34
Hawthorne, NJ 07507
1-800-CAREER-1
201-427-0229 (outside U.S.)
FAX: 201-427-2037

BUSINESS LETTERS FOR BUSY PEOPLE
SECOND EDITION
ISBN 1-56414-103-9, $14.95
Cover design by Dean Johnson Design, Inc.
Printed in the U.S.A. by Book-mart Press

To order this title by mail, please include price as noted above, $2.50 handling per order, and $1.00 for each book ordered. Send to: Career Press, Inc., 180 Fifth Ave., P.O. Box 34, Hawthorne, NJ 07507

Or call toll-free 1-800-CAREER-1 (Canada: 201-427-0229) to order using VISA or MasterCard, or for further information on books from Career Press.

Library of Congress Cataloging-in-Publication Data

Dugger, Jim.
Business letters for busy people : more than 130 time-saving, ready-to-use business letters for any occasion / by Jim Dugger. -- 2nd ed.
p. cm.
ISBN 1-56414-103-9 : $14.95
1. Commercial correspondence--Handbooks, manuals, etc. I. Title.
HF5726.D8 1993
651.7'5--dc20 93-22807
CIP

Table of Contents

Preface

Why do we call this a Business User's Manual? Because it's designed to be used, not just read. In a Business User's Manual, you not only get the easy-to-read impact of chapter-by-chapter "how to" information, but each section is also filled with checklists, ready-to-use letters and guidelines to help you do your job better, more effectively, more easily — right now! It's literally a user's manual for the business professional.

Business Letters for Busy People is written in the best-selling style of our desktop handbooks. That series has sold over a million copies because each book is packed with real-world ideas you can use. In this series, like the handbooks, we've packed the most concrete information, useful techniques and practical tips possible in the smallest space. So you don't have to wade through endless pages of fluff searching for that elusive kernel of wisdom.

The Business User's Manual series gives you concise, easy-to-use learning resources that get results. Check out the format and don't be surprised if you find yourself leafing through the pages for tidbits of fact and business trivia. Read the chapters that are immediately important to you. Although there is a logic and order to the design of the book, you can read it in the order that best suits you. Each chapter stands alone.

We know you'll find this Business User's Manual helpful. Read it, copy it and act on its advice. Reading a good book awakens our mind, but too often never gets carried into action; we close the book unchanged. But with this book, your reading becomes action. And action is the key to success.

Gary Weinberg
Vice President
National Press Publications

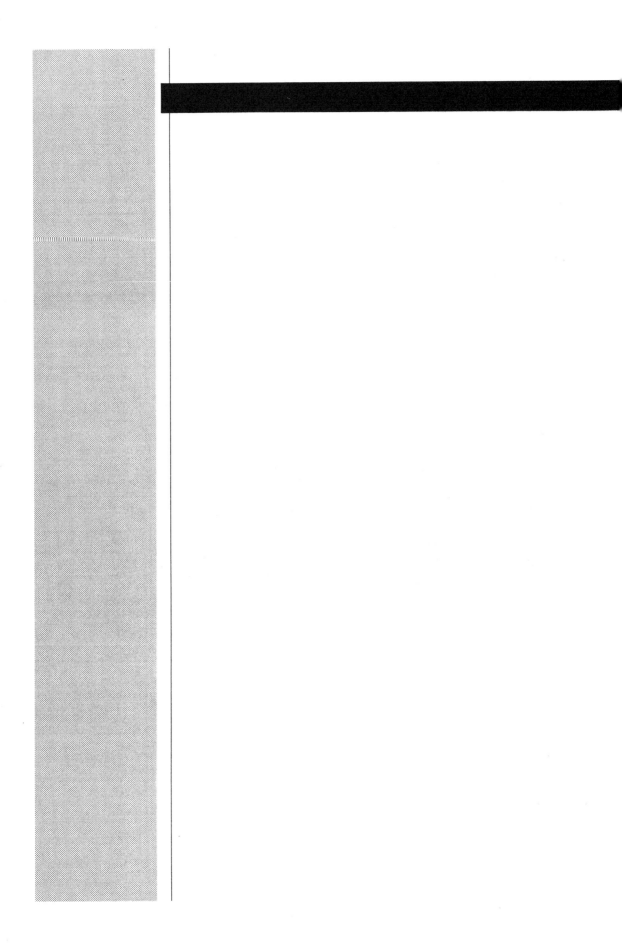

Chapter 1 — Writing from Scratch

You are busy no matter what your position. Since you are busy, you want to use your time as effectively as possible. The business letter takes time but can be written more quickly if you follow a few basic principles. (If you're in a hurry, skip to Chapters 4-9 for samples of the kinds of letters you need to write.) This chapter assumes you have a little free time to brush up on business letter writing.

Keep in mind these three points when you write a letter:

1. Business letters serve one purpose.
2. Business letters are expensive.
3. Business letters serve as a record.

Business letters serve one purpose: They communicate information. Countless hours are spent and too many letters are sent that say little or nothing. That's a waste of time for the sender and the receiver. Also, when the wages of the writer and the typist, along with the pro-rated cost of equipment and postage are figured in, business letters are expensive. It is important that they be cost-effective. Why write a business letter? Because business letters serve as a record. Letters are long-lasting, tangible evidence of information you communicate to others.

Four Considerations of a Business Letter

In a study of 800 letters written by the top chief executive officers in the U.S., all 800 letters were found to be short, clear and personal. By the time these people became CEOs, they had learned never to send out a letter that didn't reflect those three basic principles of good writing.

The four areas you must take into consideration for each business letter are listed below. If you do not consider each one of them, your letter will be ineffective.

1. Subject
2. Audience
3. Purpose
4. Style/Organization

Subject

Every piece of writing from the business letter to the novel revolves around a subject. Luckily, in the business world, the subject is usually specific and quite often supplied for you by someone else such as a boss or colleague, or demanded by a situation such as hiring or congratulating an employee.

It's a fact: The more specific your subject, the easier it is to write your letter.

For example, let's say that you need to request information about an order that did not arrive when it should have. If you are in charge of the account, writing the letter is easy. If you are not in charge of the account, it is harder for you to write the letter than it is for the person who knows all the particulars. Regardless of the situation, stick to one or two subjects in your letter. Including more than two subjects clouds your message. Write another letter if you have more than two subjects.

Audience

This area is tricky because you may not know your audience. If you do, you can tailor your letter to that audience. Many times, however, your audience is larger than you expect. Your letter may be addressed to Terry Smith, but may be read by several other people in that firm to receive the action you wish. If you are unsure of your audience, assume they are educated, reasonable people until you find out otherwise. Don't assume they have as much knowledge of the subject of your letter as you do, or you may over-generalize or forget to include important details.

The "So What?" Test

When you have finished a draft of your letter, read each paragraph and ask yourself, "So what?" in the same way a new reader might. If you can't answer that from the paragraph, consider leaving it out.

Purpose

Many letters are sent with a specific subject and audience in mind, but are not clear in their purpose.

Know why you are sending the letter. Is the letter to inform? Is it to request information? Is it to offer congratulations? Condolences? Is it to get the recipient to act on a request? All of these are very different purposes. You have probably received a letter that, after reading it, left you confused because you didn't know exactly what it said. The purpose was not clear.

Style/Organization

The first three areas dictate the content, direction and emphasis of the letter.

1. Know WHAT you're writing about — SUBJECT
2. Know WHO you're writing for — AUDIENCE
3. Know WHY you're writing — PURPOSE

Now you are ready to be concerned with HOW you are going to write the letter. The first three areas can be determined in a matter of minutes if you are familiar with the ideas that need to be communicated. The fourth area — style and organization — takes more time. (If you're pressed for time, refer to the sample letters in Chapters 4-9.)

Organization

Most of this book is devoted to the way different types of letters are organized. However, the basic organization for the body of a business letter follows:

Part 1 of Body	State your purpose.
Part 2 of Body	Explain what you want to happen or explain the information you have.
Part 3 of Body	Request action, conclude or thank the reader for his or her response.

"Brevity is the soul of wit."

— William Shakespeare

Notice these are parts or sections rather than paragraphs. In some cases, particularly Part 2, the parts may consist of more than one paragraph. Let's take a look at each of these parts.

Part 1 of the Body

Get right to the point in the first sentence of the letter. When you read a novel, you expect to have background information before the story ever starts. When you read a business letter, you expect to be told immediately what will happen. Remember, your reader doesn't have any more time to wade through a long letter than you do.

This part is usually a short paragraph. Anything too long will cause the reader to lose patience.

Part 2 of the Body

This is the bread and butter of the letter. It explains the information you are giving, or it explains what you want the recipient to do. It doesn't need to be elaborate, but it does need to include all of the information that the recipient needs.

If you have a lot of information, break it into short paragraphs, make a list or refer to an attachment. Underlining essential information is one way to highlight key points for your reader.

Your letter should be organized to help the recipient understand what to know or what to do.

"Tell 'em what you're going to say, say it, and tell 'em what you said."

Part 3 of the Body

This, like the first part, is usually a short paragraph. In writing classes, it's called the clincher — not a bad way to remember its function. Depending on the purpose of your letter, it will do one of three things.

1. **Conclude.** In an informational letter, this allows you to point out the most important item or draw all your key points into one statement.

2. **Request action.** In letters that require a response, such as collection letters, you define the action you want the recipient to take. In this part, you tell the reader what to do and when to do it. Being vague gets vague results. Be specific.

3. **Thank the reader.** In some letters, this part is simply a thank-you for the recipient's attention, response or concern.

In many ways, the method of writing a business letter is like the rule of thumb for giving a speech: Tell them what you're going to talk about it. Talk about it. Then tell them what you talked about.

Organization

The following sample letter shows how each of the three parts work:

Capital Supplies
8995 Camden Rd., Williamsburg, WI 63094

October 2, 199X

Lance Smith, Director
Terrance Trucking
P.O. Box 4440
Houston, TX 34598-4440

Dear Mr. Smith:

State Your Purpose

Thank you for your conscientious service. All 15 of your last shipments have arrived undamaged. We have never contracted with a supplier with as fine a record as yours. We appreciate the extra effort it takes to ship our order intact and on time.

Explain What You Want to Happen or Explain the Information You Have

Ted McCracken and Bob Smiley have delivered these shipments to our loading dock supervisor. I have attached copies of logs for your review. Note that the unloading time is approximately half of that from other shippers for a similar load. Ted and Bob frequently help our crew unload the crates. This additional service always comes with an exchange of jokes. Our crew collects laughs to compete with your drivers!

Request a Dated Action, Conclude, Thank the Reader

Doing business with your organization is a pleasure. You save us money by eliminating shipping waste and time by providing efficient drivers. Please accept the enclosed certificates of merit to Terrance Trucking, Ted and Bob, with our appreciation. We are confident in referring our customers and vendors to Terrance Trucking for their shipping needs.

Sincerely,

Cala Reginald
CLR:mjk
Enc. (10)

Style

Style is how you write the letter. Business letters used to be written in what might be called "businessese," a formal, stiff language. That is no longer true. The predominant style is matter-of-fact and conversational. Gone are such phrases as "the aforementioned" and "due to the fact that." Our high-tech, impersonal society requires business professionals to be more personable in our written communication in order to be more effective. The Seven "C's" of Style will help you become more effective.

The Seven "C's" of Style

"Writing, when properly managed, is but a different name for conversation."

— Laurence Sterne

1. **Conversational.** Write the way you speak. Get rid of stilted phrases. Why say "due to the fact that" when you can say "because"? Would you normally say "the aforementioned information"? Why not, "the information," or if you need to refer to a point, "the previous information"?

2. **Clear.** The goal of clarity is that the reader understands precisely what you are saying. The language of your letter should be adapted to the recipient. This means that you write in a matter-of-fact, conversational tone. Use specific examples the reader can relate to. Don't assume that your reader understands the jargon of your trade. Remember, most letters will be read by people other than the recipient of the letter. These people may be unfamiliar with the technical language or jargon you use. Clarity also means organizing your letter so each paragraph deals with only one main idea, and presenting your ideas in a logical order. Your letter should not be a collection of random ideas. It should be single-minded in its purpose.

3. **Concise.** A concise letter eliminates all unnecessary words. Why use four words, "in as much as," when you can use one word, "because"? This is not to say that you can't write long letters, but the longer the letter, the more ineffective it

becomes. It is better to write a short letter with attachments than a long, detailed one. Short letters are read and remembered; long letters are skimmed and filed.

4. **Complete.** Make sure you have included all the information the reader needs to know. Don't include details that are interesting but not relevant. The biggest problem with leaving out information is that the reader has to make assumptions. For example, don't say, "When we last spoke about the situation," when you can say, "When we spoke on June 8 about hiring a new administrative assistant."

   Remember that the reader can't read your mind. The reader can only guess at what you left out.

"Proper words in proper places make the true definition of style."

— Jonathan Swift

5. **Concrete.** Use specific terms that cannot be misunderstood. Don't say, "The large order that we requested has not arrived." Say, "The order for 10,000 basins that we requested on May 3, 199X, has not arrived as of June 20." Identify names and numbers.

   Write about what people can count or do. Include what people can see, touch, smell, taste or hear. In other words, make your language tangible. Make it concrete.

6. **Constructive.** Use words and phrases that set a positive tone. Constructive words are like smiling when you greet someone. They leave a good impression. Words such as "failure," "you neglected" and "error" tend to distance the recipient from the writer. Words such as "agreeable," "proud" and "success" help create a positive tone.

7. **Correct.** The last step in writing any business letter is to proofread it. You automatically check your image in a mirror before going out or meeting someone. The letter you

send is your image on paper. If it is riddled with spelling, grammatical and typographical errors, it will detract from what you are trying to get across. The reaction will be, “He can’t spell,” or “She doesn’t know how to type.”

If you have a secretary, don’t assume your secretary knows how to spell or punctuate. Luckily, most do; but proof your own letters. Why? Because it is your name that is signed at the bottom of the page, not your secretary’s. You will be the one who looks bad.

In a Nutshell

Writing a business letter need not be difficult as long as you remember that you are communicating with another business person just like yourself. If you incorporate Subject, Audience, Purpose and Style/Organization into your correspondence, you will be on the road to better business letter writing.

Chapter 2 — Parts of the Business Letter

2

There are many parts to the business letter, some required, some optional. This chapter will review those parts and their order. The parts of the business letter follow:

1. Letterhead or Heading
2. Date
3. File Number (optional)
4. Confidential (optional)
5. Inside Address
6. Attention Line (optional)
7. Salutation (optional)
8. Subject Line (optional)
9. Body of the Letter
10. Complimentary Close (optional)
11. Signature
12. Added Information (optional)
13. Postscripts (optional)
14. Mailing Instructions (optional)

Letterhead

Most business letters originating from a firm are written on the firm's letterhead. If you are writing a personal business letter or your firm does not use letterhead, then you need to include your firm's address in the heading (see Chapter 3 for the various formats). When you are using a heading instead of letterhead, place the date on the first line and the address on the subsequent lines as follows:

September 9, 199X
359 Longview Road
Mt. Vernon, IL 65676

Parts of the Business Letter

The standard dateline in the U.S. is month/day/year (March 15, 199X).

In Europe, however, the most widely used format is day/month/year (15 March 199X).

Date

This should be the date the letter is written. (See Chapter 3 for placement in the various formats.) Be sure to write out the month and to include both the date and year for adequate reference.

File Number

On occasion, you may wish to include such information as the file number of the project, case or order that the letter refers to. The file number should be physically separated from the date by two spaces and from the part that follows (Confidential or Inside Address) by two spaces.

Confidential

Use this word when the person to whom the letter is addressed is the only one to read the letter. Physically separate the word from the rest of the letter by two lines. To assure confidentiality, include the word "Confidential" on the envelope.

Inside Address

This should include the name of the person you are writing, the person's title if available, the name of the firm and the firm's address.

Attention Line

This is used when you do not know the name of the person you are writing and the letter is addressed to the firm. For example, the attention line may say, "Attention: Head of Accounting." It may also be used when you know the name of the person you are writing but are unsure of the title. The attention line may say, "Attention: Customer Service," thus indicating to the person receiving the letter that the letter also needs to be routed to the Customer Service department. Another way of doing this is to use the attention line and send copies of the letter to the appropriate department.

People don't usually get upset if you don't address them with the proper salutation, but they notice and appreciate it when you do.

Salutation

The salutation is used in all formats (see Chapter 3) except the Simplified Letter and the Memo. The following are salutations used in American business letters:

- Dear Sir:
- Dear Madam: (may be followed by title, such as Dear Madam Chairperson:)
- Gentlemen:
- Ladies:
- Dear Mr. Bryan:
- Dear Ms. Gray:
- Ladies and Gentlemen:
- Dear Personnel Director: (a gender-free title)
- To Whom It May Concern: or
  TO WHOM IT MAY CONCERN:
  (use this form as a last resort)

Caution:
You must determine the appropriate choice, given your reader and the situation. If you are uncertain about your reader's gender, avoid assuming gender in the salutation. Use your reader's name whenever you know it. Researchers discovered that people are more likely to read a letter with their names in the salutation.

Parts of the Business Letter

One of the problems you may run into is writing to a person with a name that is not gender specific; for example, the name Terry. The simplest solution in the salutation is to say, "Dear Terry Lucas." If you are addressing a group of people in general, such as the shipping department, do not assume that they are all male. The old "Gentlemen:" is not acceptable. "Shipping Agents" is preferred. The way around having to use a salutation when you are unsure of whom you are writing is to use the Simplified Letter (see Chapter 3).

Unless you're aiming for the Nobel prize, you shouldn't worry about your writing talent. Writing good business documents is a craft, not an art. It requires skill, not talent, and you can learn skills.

Subject Line

The subject line is most commonly used in the Simplified Letter. It announces the subject of the letter and provides a summary of your intent.

Body of the Letter

This is where you make requests, provide information or reasons or reply to someone. It is the main part of the business letter. (See Chapter 3 for the various body formats.)

Complimentary Close

This varies in formality and is found in all business letters with the exception of the Simplified and the Memo. (See Chapter 3 for its placement.) The following complimentary closes are in order of decreasing formality:

- Very truly yours,
- Respectfully,
- Sincerely yours,
- Cordially,
- Sincerely,

The most appropriate in general situations is the last.

Signature

There should be four lines between the complimentary close (or the body in the Simplified Letter) and your typed name so there is room for your signature.

Additional Information

If needed, this consists of the sender's initials in capital letters followed by a colon, followed by the typist's initials in small letters. You may also find the abbreviations "Enc." for enclosure and "cc:" or "xc:" for copies sent followed by names of persons receiving the copies.

Postscripts

The "P.S." highlights additional information that might have been placed in the letter but for some reason was not. Often used in sales, promotional or personal letters, the postscript can emphasize a request for action or consideration. It is often the first thing the recipient reads. Use it to entice or motivate your reader. Postscripts are especially effective in sales or form letters.

Studies have shown that postscripts, particularly when handwritten, are often the first thing read and the first thing remembered. Be careful, however, that what you put in a postscript isn't so important that it makes you look forgetful or careless.

Mailing Instructions

Use these to give the reader deadlines or pertinent information on mailing a reply.

As you look through the major formats in Chapter 3, it's obvious that many of the parts listed above are not necessarily used in routine business correspondence. However, it helps to be aware of all of them in case you need to use any of them.

Chapter 3 — Format of the Business Letter

3

Business letter formats have changed over the years. If you went to school prior to the 1970s, you probably learned one basic form of business letter now called the Modified Semi-block. It was the bane of every beginning typist because of its strict rules concerning spacing. Luckily, the movement in business has been to simplify and provide choices. Now you have a choice of six different forms, some extremely simple, others more complex. This chapter will review the various forms. The six forms of business letters most commonly used are:

- Block
- Modified Block
- Modified Semi-block
- Simplified
- Hanging Indented
- Memo

It is likely that your organization may prefer one form over another. In the following explanations, the assumption is that you will be using letterhead stationery. If you are writing a personal business letter without letterhead, place your address one line above or below the date as in the following examples:

August 3, 199X		2578 Tarrymore Lane
	OR	Chicago, IL 66557-1234
2578 Tarrymore Lane		
Chicago, IL 66557-1234		August 3, 199X

The state in the sender's address and the inside address may be written out in a formal letter or abbreviated with the two-letter postal service code in an informal letter. As the postal service's recommendation to use the new format for envelope addresses gains momentum, we will see another change in the business letter: The inside address may match the envelope address to eliminate the need for two separate data bases for address styles. Both can look like this:

2578 TARRYMORE LANE
CHICAGO IL 66557-1234

All letters are capitalized and no line punctuation is used, which allows the electronic scanners to sort the mail more quickly. The nine-digit ZIP code is also gaining popularity to process and deliver mail more quickly.

Format of the Business Letter

Block

The Block format is by far the simplest. Every part of the letter starts at the left margin with spaces between each part. It has a professional look to it. The order for the parts of the letter are date, inside address, salutation, body, complimentary close, signature and additional information.

Letterhead	***Italics Unlimited*** ***231 W. 40th Street • Camden, NJ 08618 • (623) 555-2678***
Date (2-3 spaces)	August 10, 199X
File Number	XXX
Inside Address (2-3 spaces)	Terry Lancaster Capital Supply 657 Minden Ct. Des Moines, Iowa 54687
Attention Line (2-3 spaces)	Attention: President of Capital Supply
Salutation (2-3 spaces)	Dear Mr. Lancaster:
Subject Line	Subject: XXXXXXXX
Body (2 spaces between para-graphs)	XXXXXXXXXXXXXXXXXXXXXXXXXXXXXXXXXXXXXX XXXXXXXXXXXXXXXXXXXXXXXXXXXXXXXXXXX XXXXXXXXXXXX XXXXXXXXXXXXXXXXXXXXXXXXXXXXXXXXXX XXXXXXXXXX
Complimentary Close (4 spaces for signature)	Sincerely,
Typed Name (2-3 spaces)	Joan McAllister
Additional Information	JFM:ecr
Postscript	P.S. XXXXXXXXX
Mailing Instructions	XXXXXXXXX

Modified Block

Like the Block, the Modified Block has the advantage of separating paragraphs so that each one stands out. The spacing between sections remains the same as in the Block. The date, signature and closing are placed to the right, thus allowing them to stand out. The complimentary close and the signature are aligned and placed near the center of the letter, two spaces below the last paragraph.

Italics Unlimited
231 W. 40th Street • Camden, NJ 08618 • (623) 555-2678

August 10, 199X

Terry Lancaster
Capital Supply
657 Minden Ct.
Des Moines, Iowa 54687

Dear Mr. Lancaster:

XXXXXXXXXXXXXXXXXXXXXXXXXXXXXXXXXXXXXX
XXXXXXXXXXXXXXXXXXXXXXXXXXXXXXXXXXX
XXXXXXXXXXXX

XXXXXXXXXXXXXXXXXXXXXXXXXXXXXXXXXXXXX
XXXXXXXXXXXXXXXXXXXXXXXXXXXXXXXXXX
XXXXXXXXXX

Sincerely,

Joan McAllister

JFM:eer

Letterhead

Date
(right of center)

Inside Address
(left margin)

Salutation
(2-3 spaces)

Body
(left margin with two spaces between paragraphs)

Complimentary Close
(right of center)

Signature
(right of center)

Additional Information
(left margin)

Format of the Business Letter

Modified Semi-block

"I hate quotations. Tell me what you know."

— Ralph Waldo Emerson

You will recognize the Modified Semi-block as the format most commonly taught as "the business letter." It is the same as the Modified Block except that the paragraphs are indented five spaces. All spacing remains the same.

Letterhead

Italics Unlimited
231 W. 40th Street • Camden, NJ 08618 • (623) 555-2678

Date (right of center)

August 10, 199X

Inside Address (left margin)

Terry Lancaster
Capital Supply
657 Minden Ct.
Des Moines, Iowa 54687

Salutation

Dear Mr. Lancaster:

Body (indent paragraphs five spaces and separate paragraphs with two spaces)

XXXXXXXXXXXXXXXXXXXXXXXXXXXXXXXXXX XXXXXXXXXXXXXXXXXXXXXXXXXXXXXXXXXX XXXXXXXXXXXX

XXXXXXXXXXXXXXXXXXXXXXXXXXXXXXXX XXXXXXXXXXXXXXXXXXXXXXXXXXXXXXXXXX XXXXXXXXXX

Complimentary Close (right of center)

Sincerely,

Signature (right of center)

Joan McAllister

Additional Information (left margin)

JFM:eer

Simplified Letter

This is useful when you do not know the title of the person you are writing to, or when you are writing to a company, government agency or organization. It eliminates the courtesy titles (Mr., Mrs., Ms., Dr.), the salutations and the complimentary close. The focus of the letter is on the body and what is to be said. The spacing is the same as the block format.

Italics Unlimited
231 W. 40th Street • Camden, NJ 08618 • (623) 555-2678

August 10, 199X

Terry Lancaster
Capital Supply
657 Minden Ct.
Des Moines, Iowa 54687

SUBJECT: PRINTING SUPPLIES

XXXXXXXXXXXXXXXXXXXXXXXXXXXXXXXXXXXXX
XXXXXXXXXXXXXXXXXXXXXXXXXXXXXXXXXXX
XXXXXXXXXXXX

XXXXXXXXXXXXXXXXXXXXXXXXXXXXXXXXXXXX
XXXXXXXXXXXXXXXXXXXXXXXXXXXXXXXXXX
XXXXXXXXXX

Joan McAllister

JFM:eer

Letterhead

Date

Inside Address

Subject of Letter (highlight this summary line with capitalization, bold face or underlining)

Signature

Additional Information

Format of the Business Letter

Hanging Indented Letter

On occasion you will see this form, but for all practical purposes it is seldom used. Its main advantage is that it calls attention to the body and each of the paragraphs. Spacing between the lines and sections is the same as in previous examples.

Letterhead	*Italics Unlimited* *231 W. 40th Street • Camden, NJ 08618 • (623) 555-2678*
Date (2-3 spaces)	August 10, 199X
Inside Address (2-3 spaces)	Terry Lancaster Capital Supply 657 Minden Ct. Des Moines, Iowa 54687
Salutation	Dear Mr. Lancaster:
Body (indent second and subsequent lines in each paragraph)	XXXXXXXXXXXXXXXXXXXXXXXXXXXXXXXXXXXXX XXXXXXXXXXXXXXXXXXXXXXXXXXXXXXXXXXXX XXXXXXXXXXXXXXXXXXXXXXXXXXX XXXXXXXXXXXXXXXXXXXXXXXXXXXXXXXXXXXXX XXXXXXXXXXXXXXXXXXXXXXXXXXXXXX XXXXXXXXXX
Complimentary Close (right of center)	Sincerely,
Signature (right of center)	Joan McAllister
Additional Information (left margin)	JFM:eer

Memo

A sixth form of letter is the Memo. Though used primarily as an inter-office communication, it is occasionally used as a business letter format. At the top of the Memo is indicated the date, the name(s) of the sender(s), the name(s) of the recipient(s), and the subject. The abbreviation "RE" is sometimes used instead of "Subject." This information is placed at the left margin. The body of the Memo is in block form. A signature and additional information are optional. The signature is often placed near the center with the additional information at the left margin.

MEMORANDUM

Date: August 10, 199X
To: Terry Lancaster
From: Joan McAllister
Subject: Printing Supplies

XXXXXXXXXXXXXXXXXXXXXXXXXXXXXXXXXX

XXXXXXXXXXXXXXXXXXXXXXXXXXXXXXXX
XXXXXXXXXXXXXXXXXXXXXXXX

XXXXXXXXXXXXXXXXXXXXXXXXXXXXXXXXX
XXXXXXXXXXXXXXXXXXXXXXXXXXXX
XXXXXXXXX

Joan McAllister

JFM:eer
cc: Ted Kapstein, Marsha Little

Memo Information

(2-3 spaces)

Body
(1 space between lines, 2 spaces between paragraphs)

(2-3 spaces)

Signature
(2-3 spaces)

Additional Information

Chapter 4 — Collection Letters

4

This chapter has sample collection letters you may have to write. The types of collection letters included are:

In this section, at the side of the page, you will find a brief explanation of each part of the letter. The first letter, on page 27, identifies each section of the letter. Subsequent letters identify only changes to the basic format.

Writing Collection Letters

Step-by-Step Guide

> *"Creditors have better memories than debtors."*
>
> *— Ben Franklin*

The purpose of the collection letter is to get the customer to pay an overdue bill.

Step 1: Check the spelling of the recipient's name. Use a gender-specific courtesy title only if you are certain of the recipient's gender. There is nothing more embarrassing or irritating than getting a collection letter, except getting one that is addressed improperly.

Step 2: The first part of the letter should state the situation, including the concern, the date purchased, the amount owed and the date due.

Step 3: The next part of the letter should indicate the deadline for paying the bill and any penalties that may result. You may also wish to indicate your company's policy concerning late payments, grace periods, penalties or alternative payment plans.

Step 4: The third part of the letter should indicate the consequences of not paying the bill. Initially, these may be penalties, but as the bill becomes more delinquent it may include warnings of ruined credit ratings or involvement of a collection agency.

Step 5: The final part of the letter should encourage the recipient to send full payment or to call you to arrange a payment schedule. End with good will and a positive attitude that this situation will be resolved satisfactorily.

Note: At the end of this chapter is a checklist to use when you write collection letters.

Notification

This letter is to notify the recipient that the bill is overdue.

Western Wear
2212 Boot Hill Rd. • Cheyenne, WY 82001

July 5, 199X

Ted Wilson
515 Ramey Ct.
Laramie, WY 82063

Dear Mr. Wilson:

Thank you for shopping with us. You are a valued customer. We appreciate your business and know that you want to keep your account current with us.

On May 15, 199X, you purchased $319.04 of merchandise from our store in Laramie. Your payment of $100 is now overdue.

In the credit agreement you signed, you agreed to pay off your bill in three payments. The first payment of $100 was due June 15, 199X. Please send this amount now.

Failure to pay on time may affect your ability to charge merchandise at our store. Thank you for your prompt attention.

You may call me at 800-555-9875 if you have any questions or concerns. Your continued patronage is important to us.

Sincerely,

Mary West
Credit Manager

MJW:cjl

Letterhead

Date
(2-3 spaces)
Inside Address
(2-3 spaces)

Salutation

State the Concern

State the Situation

Indicate Deadline

Indicate Consequences

Indicate Contact
Indicate Goodwill

Complimentary Close

Signature

Additional Information

Reminder

This letter reminds the reader that the bill is overdue and the payment still hasn't been received. Be careful to focus on observable behaviors and to avoid assumptions. Saying "We have not received payment" is an observable behavior. Saying "You have not sent payment" is an assumption. Stay positive.

Western Wear
2212 Boot Hill Rd. • Cheyenne, WY 82001

August 5, 199X

Ted Wilson
515 Ramey Ct.
Laramie, WY 82063

Dear Mr. Wilson:

Remind Recipient of the Situation

We have not yet received your payments. This is to remind you that both your first and second payments of $100 are now overdue. This $200 plus the balance of $119.04 is due on August 15.

Request Payment and Indicate Deadline

In the credit agreement you signed, you agreed to pay off your bill in three payments. The first payment of $100 was due June 15, 199X, the second of $100 on July 15, 199X, and the final payment of $119.04 on August 15, 199X. Please send the full amount in 10 days.

Indicate Consequences, Alternative and Contact

Failure to pay on time will affect your ability to charge merchandise at our store. If you want to discuss your account, call me at 800-555-9875. Perhaps we can arrange a more comfortable payment plan.

Indicate Goodwill

Thank you for your immediate attention.

Sincerely,

Mary West
Credit Manager

MJW:cjl

Inquiry

This letter inquires why the bill isn't being paid. It assumes that the bill is overdue. It's a good idea to follow this letter with a personal phone call inquiring about the payment delay. Often an alternative plan can be arranged to suit the recipient's current budget constraints. If another agreement is reached, send a copy of the new payment plan to the recipient. Continue to follow up letters with phone calls to maintain open communication. Keep a log of all calls.

Western Wear
2212 Boot Hill Rd. • Cheyenne, WY 82001

September 5, 199X

Ted Wilson
515 Ramey Ct.
Laramie, WY 82063

Dear Mr. Wilson:

Is there some reason you have not paid your bill of $319.04?

In the credit agreement you signed, you agreed to pay off your bill in three payments. Your total bill is now overdue. Please send $319.04 within 10 days. If you have any questions or concerns regarding this bill, please contact me at 800-555-9875 by September 10.

Failure to send the full amount by September 15 may mean that your bill will be turned over to a collection agency. Your prompt attention is urgent to protect your credit.

Sincerely,

Mary West
Credit Manager

MJW:cjl

Inquire

Indicate Deadline

Indicate Contact

Indicate Consequences

Urgency

This letter stresses the urgency of the customer taking some kind of action on the bill. It is a continuing progress report on the recipient's account. If an alternative payment plan has been reached previously, indicate the details of the agreement and the telephone contact dates to keep an accurate record of communications.

State the Situation
Indicate Grace Period (indicate alternative, if agreed)
Indicate Probable Consequences

Western Wear
2212 Boot Hill Rd. • Cheyenne, WY 82001

November 5, 199X

Ted Wilson
515 Ramey Ct.
Laramie, WY 82063

Dear Mr. Wilson:

Your bill of $319.04 is now overdue 60 days. Send $319.04 within 10 days. If you cannot send the total, please call me at 800-555-9875.

Failure to respond may mean that your bill is turned over to a collection agency. Thank you for your prompt attention.

Sincerely,

Mary West
Credit Manager

MJW:cjl

Final Notice/Ultimatum

This letter is the final notice the customer receives. It gives the customer an ultimatum: "If you do not respond, this will happen." After this letter there are no more chances.

Western Wear
2212 Boot Hill Rd. • Cheyenne, WY 82001

December 5, 199X

Ted Wilson
515 Ramey Ct.
Laramie, WY 82063

Dear Mr. Wilson:

Your bill of $319.04 is now 90 days overdue.

The total amount is due now.

If your payment in full is not received by December 10, your file will be turned over to a collection agency.

Sincerely,

Mary West
Credit Manager

MJW:cjl

State the Situation

Indicate Deadline

Indicate Consequences

Insufficient Funds

Sometimes a good customer sends a "bad" check.

Zenith Building Supplies
678 Central Parkway
Durham, NC 27715

August 13, 199X

Tim Blackwell, President
Blackwell Builders
98 Diego Dr.
Durham, NC 27713

Dear Mr. Blackwell:

Thank You
State Problem

Thank you for your July 28 payment, check #1429 for $200. Unfortunately, it was returned by your bank because of "insufficient funds."

Action Plan

I'm returning the check to you for your review. Please send a payment this week after you reconcile this matter with your bank. If we receive your payment by August 31, you will avoid accruing additional interest charges on your outstanding balance with us.

Goodwill

Your continued patronage is important to us. We appreciate your good payment record in the past year. We know that you, too, will be happy when this situation is resolved. If I may help, just call me at 1-800-555-1234.

Sincerely,

Jack Quentin

Enc.

Thank-You for Payment

A collection letter that is often neglected is the thank-you note. It can provide a reminder of both the account status and the customer's importance.

Word Trade, Inc.
5698 Adie Road • St. Ann, MO 63074

April 19, 199X

Vern Mueller
13245 Greenwood Lane
Overland Park, KS 66213

Dear Vern Mueller:

Thank you for your payment of $563.89. Your current balance is $3,000–your credit limit. A payment of $500 is due May 1.

We appreciate your attention to your account status with us. Your patronage is important to us.

If we may assist you, please contact us at 1-800-344-9000.

Sincerely,

Anita Collins
Account Executive

AC:etr

Thank You
Caution/Reminder

Appreciation

Contact Information

Lost Payment/Apology

Sometimes a bill adjustment and an apology are necessary.

Deem's Department Store
2030 Aquamarine Road
Silver Spring, MD 20904

August 4, 199X

Mrs. Franklin
5930 E. 46th St.
Colesville, MD 20901

Dear Mrs. Franklin:

Acknowledgment / Adjustment

Your patience has been bountiful. When we last spoke on Friday, I had not yet located your payment. I have credited $45.89 to your account today.

Policy / Adjustment

Our policy states that one percent interest (APR) is accrued on the last work day of the month on any account balance. However, we are withdrawing this policy for you for June 1 through August 31, during which time your account will reflect a zero-interest adjustment.

Reason

We found your check (#984, dated June 20, 199X) on our mailroom floor this morning. The envelope was torn away and the check was crumpled. We are still speculating about how it disappeared.

Benefit

To offset any inconvenience the interim bills have caused you, we are enclosing a 20-percent discount coupon for your next order. Just attach the coupon to your order and I'll personally assist you.

Thank You / Apology

Thank you for your patience, Mrs. Franklin. Please accept our warmest apology.

Sincerely,

Sybil Paxton
Customer Service Manager

SP:smm

Checklist

- ☐ Did you verify the name of the recipient?
- ☐ Was the tone of the letter firm but understanding?
- ☐ Did you state the amount owed?
- ☐ Did you state when the bill was originally due?
- ☐ Did you state the penalties, if any?
- ☐ Did you suggest an alternative payment plan?
- ☐ Did you state the grace period, if any?
- ☐ Did you state the new deadline?
- ☐ Did you summarize telephone contacts?
- ☐ Did you indicate the consequences of not paying the bill?

Chapter 5 — Sales and Promotional Letters

5

Actually, all letters are sales letters in business. You are selling a service or product as well as your image as a business. These letters intend to initiate or close a sale. The broad categories follow:

At the side of the page, you will find a brief explanation of each part of the letter. The first letter, on page 39, identifies each section of the letter. Subsequent letters identify only changes to the basic format.

Step-by-Step Guide

Sales and promotional letters are used by salespeople to set up or confirm appointments, announce sales promotions, congratulate salespeople on their successes and introduce new salespeople to their clients. The letter in and of itself is a sales tool. These letters are often more creative in content and composition than other kinds of letters.

Step 1: The first part of the letter states your purpose. Depending on the reason for writing the letter, this may vary from requesting an appointment to introducing a new salesperson. Your purpose is to stimulate the reader's interest. Identify the benefit to your recipient.

Step 2: The second part of the letter gives details or background information. This is the persuasive part of the letter. If you are making a request, then this part would give the reason for the request. For example, in a request for an appointment, the second part would set up the time for the appointment, the telephone number where you can be reached and the location of the appointment. If you are introducing a new salesperson, this part would give his or her background.

Step 3: The last part of the letter acts as a statement of desired action and as a summary reminding the recipient of the letter's general nature. In many sales and promotion letters, this is a thank-you; in others it is a re-statement of what has been said previously. It may also be used to summarize the details of an appointment. Many sales letters include a handwritten postscript to emphasize urgency or a benefit.

Note: At the end of this chapter is a checklist to use when you write a sales and promotion letter.

Request for Appointment

This letter is used by the salesperson to set up appointments and to announce his or her schedule. Include an added service or an "extra effort" to encourage the recipient to see you later. It is an introductory letter and should be followed up with another letter or phone call.

Carrington's 38 E. 91st St. • Chicago, IL 60614	**Letterhead**
January 25, 199X	**Date**
Linda Montgomery, Manager A-1 Cleaners 2903 Burresh St. Lincoln, NE 68506	**Inside Address**
Dear Ms. Montgomery:	**Salutation**
I will be in Lincoln on February 3 and would like to meet with you at your office to discuss cleaning supplies that you may need in the second half of the year.	**Request for Appointment**
I have enclosed our latest catalog. Please note the items in yellow highlight. They are special values or new products that A-1 Cleaners will want to take advantage of now.	**Benefit** **Added Service**
I will contact you later this week to schedule an appointment. If you need to get in touch with me, call me at 800-555-9047. I look forward to talking with you. Thank you for your continued business.	**Confirmation** **Thank You**
Sincerely yours,	**Complimentary Close**
Douglas James Sales Representative	**Signature** **Title**
DNJ:llr Enc.	**Additional Information**
P.S. See page 68 of our catalog for a great value on your most-ordered product choice!	**Postscript**

Prospect Lead

This letter is a follow-up from a lead given to the salesperson. It introduces the salesperson to the prospective lead.

TOM'S SPORT SUPPLY
665 Spinning Wheel Ct., Bilmont, UT 84106

December 4, 199X

Terrance O'Toole
Golfers Teed Off
870 C. Street
Walla Walla, WA 98661

Dear Mr. O'Toole:

Purpose
Reference
Added Service

You and your firm have been recommended by Cal Gonzonles of Fore, Inc. Cal indicated that you may be interested in the line of products that we have, particularly our new Golflite line. I have enclosed our latest catalog.

Request for Appointment
Contact Information

I will be in the Walla Walla area the week of December 16. I would like to meet with you to discuss how our Golflite line can help your business. I will contact you within the next 10 days to schedule an appointment. In the meantime, if you have any questions, call me at 1-800-555-1125. I look forward to meeting you.

Sincerely yours,

Chip Ashcroft
Sales Representative

CNA:pam
Enc.

Letter of Introduction

This letter is used to introduce one person to another — such as a new salesperson to an established client. If you address the recipient by first name, you can do likewise with the person being introduced. If a courtesy title and a last name are more appropriate, be consistent with all the names that are mentioned in the salutation, body and closing signature.

SEA LANES
8945 N. Shore Dr. • Boston, MA 01611 • 1-800-555-3456

November 22, 199X

Carl N. White
Lobster Trappers Ltd.
Box 65
Kepaquadick Cove, ME 04103

Dear Carl:

I am happy to introduce our new sales representative, Terry King, to you. Terry will be in charge of servicing your account.

Terry is a graduate of the University of Maine and holds a degree in Sales and Marketing. For the last five years he has worked as a salesman for Boston Fisheries and Equipment. We are proud to have him on our staff and are sure he will be able to give you the kind of service you have come to expect from Sea Lanes.

Please call us if there is anything that we can do for you. Terry will be contacting you within the next two weeks to personally introduce himself, discuss his monthly schedule and answer any questions you might have. Ask Terry about his family's secret recipe for lobster!

Sincerely yours,

T.K. (Tip) Walton
Director of Sales

TKW:joi

Introduction
Reason

Background Information

Support

Request
Contact Information

Personal Note

Follow-Up on Letter Sent

This letter asks the customer if he or she has received a letter.

Three W's
Box 231 • Medford, MO 64506

December 1, 199X

Caldonia Patterson
789 Winterwood Lane
St. Joseph, MO 64503

Dear Ms. Patterson:

Reference

On November 10, I sent you a letter describing our newest product. Did you receive the letter?

Purpose

I will be happy to answer any questions you may have and explain the unique features of Vu-More and its benefits to you.

Compliment Assistance Offer and Contact Information

You are a valued customer and if there is any way that I can help you in making a decision, please call me at 1-800-555-1309.

Sincerely,

Kay Lynne Overmeyer
Sales Director

KLO:pst

Delinquent Reply

This letter is used to remind a customer who has not responded to a recent letter.

LAKELAND INSURANCE
7779 23rd St. E., Camden, NJ 08610

October 2, 199X

Barry Wu
Wu's Gardens
558 Magnolia
Garden City, NJ 08638

Dear Mr. Wu:

Just a reminder: I recently sent you a computer printout of a proposal of health insurance for your employees.

I have attached another printing for your convenience and hope that you will take the time to review it. As you can see, we offer a competitive package. Plans A and B are especially responsive to your needs.

I will call you next Friday, after you have had time to review the proposal. I am eager to do business with you. In the meantime, if you have any questions or concerns, I can be reached at 308-555-9847.

Sincerely,

Terry Laforge
Sales Manager

TML:wie
Enc.

Reminder

Review

Emphasis

Assistance Offer

Contact Information

Extremely Delinquent Reply

This letter is used when a customer has not responded after a long period of time.

CATTLEMAN'S
3567 Hereford Lane • Tulsa, OK 73072

July 15, 199X

J.M. Chesterman
900 Oilman Highway
Tinderbox, CO 80215

Dear Mr. Chesterman:

Statement of the Situation

Yesterday I was going through our files and realized that we had neglected to contact you concerning our proposal to replace your cattle feeders.

Reference

Benefits

I realize that four months have passed since I sent you the information, so I have attached our original proposal. I hope you will take time to look it over. We feel our prices are very competitive and the quality and durability of our feeders will actually save you money in the long term.

Contact Information

I will call you next Monday, after you have had time to review the proposal. I am looking forward to doing business with you. If you have any questions or concerns, I can be reached at 308-555-9847.

Sincerely,

Theodore "Tex" Miller
President

TJM:ssm
Enc.

Postscript

P.S. You can save $535 on a feeder this year!

Requesting Customer's Assistance

This letter is used as a foot in the door and to request that a potential customer help the salesperson.

Martin Medical
3445 Medford Ave., Charleston, SC 29624

March 17, 199X

Terrance Reilly
Box 557
Camden Creek, SC 29625

Dear Mr. Reilly:

I would like your help in solving a problem that people in businesses such as yours have.

Each year businesses that sell medical supplies are faced with hundreds of new products. We would like your assistance in answering the enclosed survey. By doing so you will let us know how we can best serve you. Also, enclosed is a 10%-off coupon to use on your next order to thank you for your time. I'll call you on Wednesday to ask your opinions concerning the survey.

We value people like you who are willing to take their time to help us serve our customers better. Thanks for all your help.

Sincerely yours,

Jack Larimer
Sales Manager, 800-555-3590

JKL:jiw
Enc.

P.S. The coupon is good now!

Assistance Request

Background Information

Added Service

Thank You

Postscript

Sales Follow-Up

This letter is used to follow up on a sale that has been made. It may be a thank-you for the business, a clarification of the sale or a pitch for future sales.

UNLIMITED VIEW
1854 Vision Lane, Arlington, TX 76016

February 15, 199X

Marlene T. Thompson
Director of Sales
Omni-Optical Co.
334 S. 114th Avenue
Dallas, TX 75218

Dear Ms. Thompson:

Statement of Sales

Congratulations on your outstanding sales during our recent winter campaign. Omni-Optical sold 23 percent of our total volume during this program. Please commend your sales staff for their impressive efforts.

Request

Added Service

Thank You

Goodwill

Because of your success, you now qualify for our quantity discount. Thanks again for your efforts. We look forward to sharing future sales successes with Omni-Optical.

Sincerely,

J. Kelly Bandman
Sales Representative

JKB:yek

Reminder That a Sale is About to End

Remind a customer that a sale or sales campaign is about to end.

Myrna's Furniture Mart
709 Downey Road • Wiltonshire, NH 03068

April 25, 199X

Grant W. Werner
Rural Habitats
R.R. 3
Wiltonshire, NH 03104

Dear Mr. Werner:

It hardly seems possible, but there is only one week left in our annual Eastertide Sale. Our letter announcing the sale arrived four weeks ago. It seems like yesterday.

It's still not too late to take advantage of this gigantic sale. The prices this last week are being slashed in half. Come in and take a look at what we have to offer. Our entire sales staff is ready to work with you and Rural Habitats.

Attached is our Eastertide Sale flyer. Please take time to look it over and then come see us. You will be glad you did.

Sincerely,

Myrna L. Meyerhoff
Sales Manager

MLM:kwn
Enc.

P.S. See the special offer on Page 2 of the flyer!

First Reminder

Review

Added Service

Second Reminder

Announcing a Sales Campaign, Promotion or Incentive Program

This type of letter informs clients of an upcoming sales promotion, incentive program or special sales packages that are available. It is followed by a personal call from the salesperson

UNLIMITED VIEW
1854 Vision Lane • Arlington, TX 76016

September 15, 199X

Marlene T. Thompson
Director of Sales
Omni-Optical Co.
334 S. 114th Ave.
Dallas, TX 75218

Dear Ms. Thompson:

Announcement

Unlimited View will start its winter sales campaign on November 1.

Explanation

Benefits

Added Service

In the past, this campaign has enabled Omni-Optical to offer its customers a wide selection of products at very competitive prices. It is an outstanding way to attract new customers and build traffic for your business. I have enclosed a sheet explaining all of the particulars along with our latest catalogue.

Deadline

Thank You

I will call you within the next 10 days to answer any questions you have about the program and take your order. All orders have to be in by October 15. As always, it is a pleasure working with Omni-Optical.

Sincerely yours,

J. Kelly Bandman
Sales Representative

JKB:yek

Announcing a Sales Campaign to Preferred Customers

Announce a sales campaign to preferred customers, thus giving them a head start in purchasing, or offering them further reduced prices.

Green Mountain Antiques Wholesale
Stapleton, VT 05020

January 19, 199X

Max Castle
Heavenly Daze Antiques
Wiloughby, NH 03308

Dear Mr. Castle:

Green Mountain Antiques Wholesale will hold its Winter Sale February 12-16. — **Announcement**

As a preferred customer, you are invited to attend a pre-sale showing on February 11 with discounts up to 50% on specially marked items. We feel that this is just one small way that we can repay you for all your business over the years. Our enclosed flyer shows you some of the outstanding values available. — **Elaboration** / **Effective Date** / **Benefit**

Thank you for your business. I hope we will see you on February 11. — **Thank You**

Sincerely,

Madeline O'Shea

MAO:ser
Enc.

Announcing New Products to Select Group of Customers

Announce new products to a select group of regular customers. It may be seen as a sales pitch.

Ft. Dodge Appliances
563 Grand Ave., Ft. Dodge, IA 50569

October 30, 199X

Caroline M. Ness
R.R. 3
Gowrie, IA 50337

Dear Ms. Ness:

Announcement

Ft. Dodge Appliances is pleased to announce our new line of Wonder Work Appliances. We are now the authorized Wonder Work dealer for Ft. Dodge.

Elaboration

Added Service

Benefits

Wonder Work Appliances, established for three decades in the East, is now expanding to the Midwest, and we are excited to be part of its expanding network. It specializes in small appliances that are known throughout the industry for their quality and durability. So that you may have a chance to see the appliances at work, we have arranged to demonstrate them this Saturday, November 3, at our store from 9 to 5. Special discounts are available if you bring this letter.

Thank You

Thank you for your continued business. We look forward to seeing you this Saturday.

Sincerely,

Barney Carlson

BAC:eeo

Announcing a Price Increase

Announce a price increase and soften the blow to the customer.

GRAND GREETINGS, INC.
330 Big Bend St., Charleston, SC 29410

February 22, 199X

Harry C. Marker
Card Distributors, Ltd.
11 Fillmore
Atlanta, GA 30325

Dear Mr. Marker:

Your satisfaction is important to us. In order to continue to produce a high-quality product, we have recently installed new high-speed, high-definition printing presses. This, along with the increased price of paper, has forced us to increase our prices by 10 percent effective March 15. I have enclosed a brochure with the new prices in it for your benefit. Orders received before March 15 will be filled at current prices.

Thank you for your understanding in this matter. We feel that these increases will still allow you to sell these superb cards at competitive prices. We hope you will let us know immediately if there is any way we may serve you better.

Sincerely,

K. Charles Grand
President

KCG:lpw
Enc.

Goal of Customer Satisfaction

Announcement

Incentive

Thank You

Goodwill

Transmittal with Instructions

Complicated instructions can be handled in a cover letter such as this one. Part of each sale is to get the reader/buyer to perform an action that brings him or her closer to the close of the sale or resale.

ZARCON LASER SYSTEMS
80000 Orange Blossom Dr.
Boston, MA 02174

March 15, 199X

Tony Blumenthal, Realtor
The Winstead Building, Suite 400
P.O. Box 46758
Boston, MA 02180

Dear Tony:

Purpose
Enclosures

Two copies of the revised six-month leasing agreement for the Zarcon Laser Copier II are enclosed. I'm pleased you are happy with its performance.

Instruction

The yellow highlights on one copy reflect the changes that we addressed in our March 14 conversation. Please indicate any additions or omissions in the margins, and initial and date each correction. I will review the copy and get back to you by April 5.

Alternate Instruction

If the current changes meet with your approval, please sign at the "X" on page 3 of the unmarked copy and return it in the SASE by March 29.

Contact Information

If I may clarify or help in any other way, Tony, please call me at 788-3993.

Sincerely,

Lee Webster
Senior Account Executive

Enc.

Transmittal with Request

When you must send material and make a request for other material, use a cover letter such as this. Each exchange of information is part of the sales strategy. Keep all technical discussions brief in the letter with further explanation in the enclosures.

ROCKY FLATS PHYSICS FACILITY
2367 Central Avenue
Albuquerque, NM 87106

February 16, 199X

Joseph P. Harlow, PhD
Defense Engineering
784 Trinity Dr.
Los Alamos, NM 87544

Dear Dr. Harlow:

Your inquiry regarding our services is welcome. I am enclosing a brochure that will summarize our optics program for infra-red conductors and the surface lab work we do.

If you will send us similar literature from your agency, I can be more specific about what we can do for you.

I will call you later this week to answer any questions. Thank you for your interest.

Sincerely,

Zack A. Bromley, PhD

Enc.

Response to Inquiry

Request Benefit

Contact Information

Transmittal with Suggestion

This letter covers technical information briefly and refers to additional service possibilities. Again, allow the enclosures to handle the details of technical material. Use the cover letter to summarize or highlight only.

William Hennings Accountants
Drawer NN
Burlington, NC 27216

December 10, 199X

Linda Maple
77 Cherry Brook Terr.
Burlington, NC 27218

Dear Linda:

Response to Request

Your projection for the possible grantor-retained income trust (GRIT) is included with this letter.

Added Service

You may also want to investigate grantor-retained annuity trusts (GRATS) and grantor-retained unitrusts (GRUTS). I have taken the liberty of including a pamphlet describing these options in more detail.

Assistance Offer

Please let me know if I may clarify anything for you. We could meet any time next Thursday at your convenience to discuss which trusts best suit your assets and family situation.

Sincerely,

Davis C. Cerniceck

Enc.

Writing Sales and Promotional Letters

Checklist

- ☐ Did you use a positive tone?
- ☐ Does the letter sell itself?
- ☐ Did you introduce the topic of the letter in the first part?
- ☐ Did you mention the recipient's accomplishment or benefit early?
- ☐ Did you include all of the necessary details for the client such as date, time and place of appointment?
- ☐ Did you include a telephone number so that the client can reach you?
- ☐ Did you take the initiative in the letter for the action you desire?
- ☐ Did you include all background information, added service or details necessary in the second part of the letter so that the client understands the letter?
- ☐ Did you summarize, thank or recongratulate in the last part of the letter?
- ☐ If you received the letter, would you do what you are asking the recipient to do?

Chapter 6 — Goodwill Letters

This chapter has sample letters to help you write goodwill letters. The broad categories are Professional Recognition and Company Position. These letters identify special events, achievements and issues.

Professional Recognition includes:

Company Position includes:

Other goodwill letters follow in Chapters 7 and 8.

At the side of the page, you will find a brief explanation of each part of the letter. The first letter, on page 59, identifies each section of the letter. Subsequent letters will identify only changes to the basic format.

Step-by-Step Guide

When asked what he thought about Western civilization, Mahatma Gandhi responded by saying, "I think it would be a very good idea."

These letters are designed to promote goodwill among clients and employees.

Step 1: The first part of the letter states your purpose. Depending on the reason for writing the letter, this may vary from complimenting an employee on an accomplishment to apologizing for being unable to attend a social event.

Step 2: The second part of the letter gives the details or background information for the first part. This may be anything from explaining to a client the action required to correct a problem to giving details about a social event.

Step 3: The last part of the letter acts as a summary, reminding the recipient of the general nature of the letter. It may be a thank-you or it may restate what has been said in the first part of the letter. For example, if the letter is congratulatory, the last part recongratulates the recipient.

Note: At the end of this chapter is a checklist to use when you write a goodwill letter.

Recognizing a Suggestion

This letter recognizes an employee or business associate for suggestions he or she has made. Recognition fulfills one of your employees' or associates' greatest personal needs. Use these letters often.

Zimmerman's Resort
Highway 131 • Moose Lake, MN 55438

June 30, 199X

Max Moehlmann
Box 25
Moose Lake, MN 55438

Dear Max:

Thank you for your great suggestion on how to organize the annual fish fry at Zimmerman's. Your idea means we can serve 100 more people than we did last year. Without a doubt, it is the single best idea that I've seen in a long time.

As you know, Zimmerman's motto is "Fun for All" and as a reward for your suggestion, we are giving you a day-long pass to Valley Faire in Shakopee, Minnesota, for you and your family. We hope you all can live up to Zimmerman's motto.

Thank you once again for your great idea. With employees like you, Zimmerman's will only get better.

Sincerely,

Sally Zimmerman
President

SJZ:dft

First Thanks

General Statement About Company(optional)

Benefit

Second Thanks
(optional)

Appreciation

This letter expresses appreciation for something that was done. Quite often these are to employees of a company. Thank-you notes are meaningful rewards. The written word has power.

SEVEN SISTERS
709 Starry Way — Council Bluffs, IA 50574

April 13, 199X

R.K. Kirkman
4590 N. Iowa Avenue
Omaha, NE 68164

Dear Mr. Kirkman:

Reason for Appreciation

On behalf of the staff at Seven Sisters, I want to express my appreciation for your help in our recent ad campaign. Your tireless efforts made the campaign one of the most successful we have ever had.

General Statement About the Company

Seven Sisters' success relies heavily on the commitment of its employees. Devotion such as yours allows us to be leaders in the field of fashion merchandising in the Omaha/Council Bluffs area.

Specific Recognition

Your efforts contribute to higher sales and that, as you know, means increased profit-sharing for our employees.

Thank You

Thank you for all of your hard work. Seven Sisters is successful because of employees like you.

Sincerely,

Laney Moore
President

LAM:rie

Official Anniversary

This letter recognizes an official anniversary such as the ordination of a priest or minister, an elected official taking office or an employee's work anniversary. It elevates morale.

Wood Hollow Cranberries
850 Random Rd., New London, CT 06320

April 8, 199X

Edward Brown
8879 Kirksville Ct.
New London, CT 06320

Dear Ed:

All of us at Wood Hollow Cranberries wish to extend our sincerest congratulations on your tenth anniversary here at Wood Hollow. Your work, first as Assistant Plant Manager and now as Plant Manager, has been exemplary. We are most pleased to have you on our management team and look forward to many more years of working with you.

Sincerely yours,

Grant Kleissman
President

GWK:gmn

Congratulations

Specific Positions

Goodwill

Speech

This letter acknowledges a speech the recipient gave and comments on it.

Coolidge High School
3222 25th St., N.E. • Minot, ND 58504

May 23, 199X

Barbara Rundle, Principal
Lake of the Woods High School
Box 66
Lake of the Woods, MN 20902

Dear Ms. Rundle:

Acknowledgment of Speech

I recently attended the North Central States Principals' Convention in Fargo and heard your speech on problems in the rural high school. I was most impressed and came away with many new ideas and insights.

Comments About the Speech

Additional Service

I was particularly interested in your discussion of college preparation in the rural school. Although Calvin Coolidge High School does not qualify as a rural school, it has many of the same problems. An author I've found most enlightening who deals with rural schools is Garret Randolf. His works, *Rural America Who's Educating You?* and *One Room Schools Grown Up*, are both excellent. Are you aware of these titles? They weren't on your bibliography.

Expectation

I shall look forward to your speech in Pierre as I see you are on the program.

Sincerely,

C. Max Hanks
Principal

CMH:bar

Invitations — Formal

This letter's formal language reflects the formality of the event. It requires a formal reply.

ERSKINS AND CO.
985 Washington, Boise, ID 83805
555-8800

October 1, 199X

Carmen and Ted Schmitt
800 Lander Lane
Meridian, ID 83642

Dear Mr. and Mrs. Schmitt:

You are cordially invited to a formal dinner in honor of Samuel Whitters on October 21, 199X, at 8 p.m. at the Boise Hilton.

As you are an associate of Mr. Whitters, Mrs. Schmitt, we would like you to speak briefly about his work in the lumber industry. If this is possible, please let me know within the next week.

Please note that this is a black-tie event. RSVP with the names of those attending by October 14.

Sincerely yours,

John Randall, III
Chairman, Social Committee

JKR:sat

Time, Date and Place of Event

Request

Deadline

Requirements

Invitations — Informal

This letter is more informal and conversational in style. It may require a reply, but the reply may be oral or informally written.

TeleWorld
1810 Ohio Ave., Little Rock, AR 72293

June 13, 199X

Ramona Jenkins
55 Tremont
Little Rock, AR 72291

Dear Ramona:

Time, Date and Place of Event

The marketing department is having a *surprise* get-together next Thursday afternoon after work for the retirement of J.J. Small.

Requests

Please bring a gag gift to send J.J. on his way to a happy retirement. We're asking each person to contribute $5 for a legitimate retirement gift. Wanda Templeman is collecting.

Requirements Deadline

Let Wanda (X. 233) know by Monday if you can make it so she can order enough refreshments.

Sincerely,

Chuck Meyers
Chairman, Social Committee

CJM:eem

Congratulations

This is a goodwill letter on the part of the company or the salesperson to a client. It congratulates an internal client on an accomplishment.

CAPITAL LIFE INSURANCE CO.
369 Wilmington Blvd., Camden, NJ 07102

May 7, 199X

Seth Tinkerton, Jr.
District Manager
839 Littleton Ct.
Morningside, NJ 07112

Dear Mr. Tinkerton:

Congratulations on being the top district manager in Capital for March and April. You can be proud of your hard work, and we're glad you work with us.

Capital Life honors its high achievers with our Call to Excellence Award. Your achievement in sales will be recognized at the June Convention in Philadelphia. We would like you and your agents to be our guests at a special banquet on June 5, 199X, at 7:30 p.m. in the Cameo Room of the Hotel International, during which you will receive the award.

Once again, congratulations! It is because of managers like you that Capital Life has achieved the success it enjoys.

Sincerely yours,

John R. Liu
Vice President

JRL:cco

Acknowledgment of Accomplishment

General Statement About Achievement

Specific Details

Re-statement

Acknowledging an Accomplishment

Similar to the congratulatory letter, this letter acknowledges an accomplishment of a client, employee, relative of a client or employee, or friend of the company.

PAMPERED PRINTS
282 Kefauver Dr., Mt. Vernon, KY 42040

March 30, 199X

Maria Fernandez
3333 Trenton Way
Mt. Vernon, KY 42049

Dear Maria:

Acknowledgment of Accomplishment

Your design for our Kute Kids line is outstanding! Pampered Prints is proud that you are one of our employees.

General Statement About Achievement

Because of your design, Kute Kids is breaking all records in sales. During the first quarter, Kute Kids outsold all other lines in the Size 6-12 category.

Encouragement

Keep up the good work. We need people like you, Maria, at Pampered Prints.

Sincerely yours,

Lily Marret
Director of Sales

LNM:ddl

Encouragement

This letter offers encouragement to the employees of a firm.

RM TRUCKING
8092 Los Noches • Santa Fe, NM 87538
505-555-0050

December 12, 199X

Cappy Kappmeier
Wind Willow 13
Santa Fe, NM 87538

Dear Cappy:

Every year I take time to look ahead to what the next year has in store for our employees. Next year's outlook is exciting.

RM Trucking in the past year has experienced phenomenal growth, moving from the tenth largest trucking firm in New Mexico to the second largest. We project that in the coming year we will become number one in New Mexico and number two in the combined states of New Mexico and Arizona. It is because of our farsighted staff that we have been able to achieve this kind of success. Naturally, this success affects everyone who works for RM Trucking. Because of our unique profit-sharing plan, each employee benefits.

Next year will be exciting at RM for all of us involved. I hope you will make the most of these opportunities.

Sincerely,

Ronald Martin
President

RMM:wan

Purpose

Explanation of the Purpose

Benefits

Restatement Encouragement

Explaining Policy and Position

This memo clarifies a company's policy and position for its employees. Normally a memo would suffice, but a formal letter may also be appropriate in certain circumstances.

MEMORANDUM

Date: December 23, 199X
To: All Employees
From: Manuel Gonzales
Re: Policy Concerning Sick Leave

Statement of the Situation

There seems to be some misunderstanding concerning Swithams' sick leave policy.

Clarification

Each employee is allowed 10 sick days per year during the first five years of employment. For five to 10 years of employment each employee is allowed 15 days of sick leave. Any employee of 10 or more years is granted 20 days of sick leave. Sick leave may be accumulated up to one full year (365 days). After an absence of two days an employee must seek medical advice and present a doctor's excuse upon return to work. Failure to do so may result in docking of pay for any sick leave after two consecutive days. For further information, refer to the employee manual, page 23, or contact our Benefits Officer, Barbara Wieland.

Evidence

Specific Issue
Goodwill

I hope this clears up any misunderstanding, particularly concerning the doctor's excuse.

Adjustment

This letter requests an adjustment, either business or social, and asks for the understanding of the person for whom the adjustment is being asked.

Australian Outfitters
P.O. Box 212 • Los Angeles, CA 99045-0212

October 3, 199X

Corbin Reynolds
3510 Aroya Canyon Road
Hollywood Hills, CA 95234

Dear Mr. Reynolds:

I regret to inform you that your order of boomerangs will be delayed by four weeks because of a recent fire at Outback Boomerangs in Sydney, Australia.

I hope this delay is acceptable. As soon as we found out, we contacted Woolabang Boomerangs in Alice Springs and were able to fill your order. Unfortunately, its boomerangs take longer to make because they are handmade. This is to your advantage: though they are more expensive, we will absorb the difference in cost.

Thank you for your understanding and cooperation in this unfortunate matter. If you have any questions, please call me at 800-OUTBACK.

Sincerely yours,

Tanner Dundee

TJD:mal

Apology
Reason

Explanation

Benefit

Thanks

Announcing New Fringe Benefits

This letter announces new fringe benefits to employees of a company.

Warwick Manufacturing
1500 Burnside Parkway, Warwick, RI 02891

August 24, 199X

Glenn Golden
90 Wuthering Heights Dr.
Kingston, RI 02881

Dear Mr. Golden:

Announcement

It is my pleasure to announce that Warwick Manufacturing is offering a new employee benefit plan starting January 1.

Explanation

Enclosure

After much discussion with management and labor, we have settled on a plan that allows you to choose those benefits you want and need. The enclosed brochure outlines the complete program. We are excited about it because you will have total control over your benefits.

Contact Information

Please call Sally Martin in the Human Resources Department if you have any questions or concerns.

Closing Statement

We hope that you will be pleased with this new benefit package.

Sincerely,

Susanna M. Graham
President

SMG: ccr

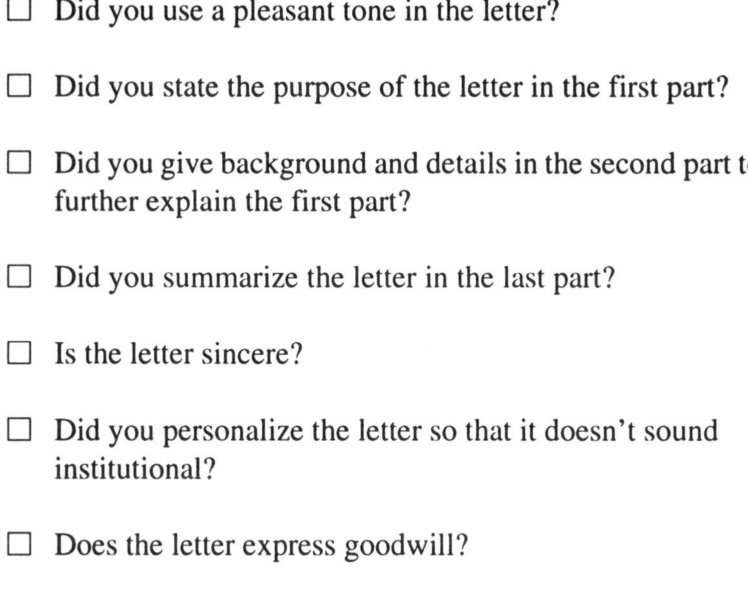

Checklist

- ☐ Did you use a pleasant tone in the letter?
- ☐ Did you state the purpose of the letter in the first part?
- ☐ Did you give background and details in the second part to further explain the first part?
- ☐ Did you summarize the letter in the last part?
- ☐ Is the letter sincere?
- ☐ Did you personalize the letter so that it doesn't sound institutional?
- ☐ Does the letter express goodwill?
- ☐ If you received the letter, would you feel good about it?

Chapter 7 — Community Activities Letters

This chapter has sample letters dealing with community activities. The broad categories are as follows:

At the side of the page, you will find a brief explanation of each part of the letter. The first letter, on page 75, identifies each section of the letter. Subsequent letters identify only changes to the basic format.

Writing Community Activities Letters

Step-by-Step Guide

These letters address community activities that involve both individuals and corporations.

Step 1: The first part of the letter states your purpose. It may vary from asking a company to take part in a charity fundraising drive to expressing appreciation for an employee's involvement in the community.

Step 2: The second part of the letter gives the details or background information for the first part. This may include giving a reason for declining a public office to indicating your company's policy about an employee's achievement.

Step 3: The last part of the letter acts as a summary, reminding the recipient of the general nature of the letter. It may include deadlines, a thank-you, or a re-request.

Note: At the end of this chapter is a checklist to use when you write a community activities letter.

Solicitation of Funds

This letter requests that a company contribute to a charity.

JJT: HEAVY EQUIPMENT **1288 E. U.S. 63 • Sioux City, IA 50585**	Letterhead
April 9, 199X	Date
William J. Buchheit President Sanders and Thoms 348 Lincolnway Dr. South Sioux City, IA 50585	Inside Address
Dear Mr. Buchheit:	Salutation
The United Benefit for Community Improvement is starting its annual drive this Monday. We hope you will contribute to this worthy cause.	Request
In the past, Sanders and Thoms has been one of the leaders in the UBCI drive, with its employees giving an average of 2.5% of their income to the fund. Naturally, they recognize that the fund improves their lives as well as the lives of others in the area. May we count on your corporate support again? This year we are asking each corporation to match their employees' contributions.	Support or Background Information Recognition
Your contributions provide recreation scholarships to summer and after-school programs for youth, home maintenance assistance for the elderly, AIDS education, a community pantry and kitchen and other programs for community improvement.	Benefit
Please continue your leadership in community development through your support of UBCI. We are asking that all contributions, employee and corporate, be in the UBCI office, 3001 Carrington Way, Sioux City, Iowa, 56884, by May 15. Thank you for your continued support.	Re-request, Deadline and Thanks
Sincerely yours,	Complimentary Close
Lannie Miller Campaign Chairperson	Signature
LJM:wit	Additional Information

Solicitation of Funds

An initial information letter is necessary to introduce the non-profit organization to the reader. This information should appeal to both emotion and intellect for the greatest impact.

HAVEN HOME
P.O. Box 124 • Memphis, TN 38124

March 12, 199X

Dear Friend,

Story

Jenny Louise is 12 years old. Her parents argued last month. The shotgun blast ignited the heater and her father died in the explosion. Her mother is still hospitalized with severe burns. Jenny Louise was lucky — at least physically. She was placed at Haven Home because no foster parents are available to care for her now. Our community resources are stretched to capacity.

Statistics

Thousands of children face the consequences of domestic violence each day. Families suffer, children cry and people die. Unresolved, unrestrained anger is at epidemic proportions in most urban communities today. Memphis is included. Within the past 12 months, Haven Home has received 3,122 crisis calls, sheltered 738 individuals and educated 20,493 concerned people.

Appeal for Volunteers and Funds

Individuals like Jenny Louise who seek our help need your help. Please consider a donation of time or money — or both. No matter how much of either you have, you have more of each than those at Haven Home.

Time: Apply to be a foster parent through the state human resources agencies. Call us for information or an appointment to contribute your time as a volunteer at Haven Home.

Money: $20 pays one person's meals for a day; $50 pays a week's utilities; $100 trains an adult in anger control or prepares a person for the G.E.D.

Send as much as you can now. Together we can make a difference!

Sincerely,

Anna Phelps
Executive Director

AP:sfg

Postscript

P.S. Make your tax deductible check payable to Haven Home. Thank you!

Acknowledgment and Request for Funds

Follow-up letters provide a non-profit organization the opportunity to thank a contributor and to suggest future contributions.

HAVEN HOME
P.O. Box 124 • Memphis, TN 38124

March 25, 199X

Doris Pearson
278 Briarwell St.
Memphis, TN 38121

Dear Doris:

Thank you for your generous donation. Your contribution of $50 will enable us to continue helping our community fight against domestic violence.

Would you consider giving Haven Home a monthly donation of $50? Our needs continue throughout the year and we count on the generosity of people such as you, Doris. Other ways you might consider to help us secure our programs for the future include memorials, trusts, scholarships and bequests. With your financial support and our dedicated volunteers, Haven Home can continue to serve victims of domestic violence with high quality intervention programs.

Again, thank you for your support.

Sincerely,

Anna Phelps
Executive Director

AP:sfg

Thank You Acknowledgment

Continuing Need and Appeal

Thank You

Appreciation and Fundraising Event

Contributors want to know how their dollars are used. Updating a previous story is one way to show value. Another way is through an appreciation event that may or may not be connected to additional fundraising.

HAVEN HOME
P.O. Box 124 • Memphis, TN 38124

May 5, 199X

Doris Pearson
278 Briarwell St.
Memphis, TN 38121

Dear Doris:

Thanks / Appreciation

Thank you! Your pledge for $25 each month for a year is greatly appreciated.

Specific Response

You asked about an update regarding Jenny Louise: She and her mother are now living with her maternal grandmother and the investigation around the explosion continues. Thank you for your concern.

Suggestions

Appreciation

Many people have expressed their concern and commitment to stop domestic violence through their pledges and gifts. Some have volunteered as a result. The Board, staff, volunteers, and residents at Haven Home want to thank you each in person. Please join us for an appreciation dinner supported by

Event Details

> Georgio's Fine Italian Restaurant
> at 39th Street and Knoll
> on Thursday, May 23, 199X at 7:30 p.m.

Fundraising Event

A silent auction will follow dinner. Retail stores at the Galla Center are donating items for our event. We would be delighted to have you attend.

Thanks

As always, thank you for your help.

Sincerely,

Anna Phelps
Executive Director

AP:sfg

RSVP

RSVP by May 20 at 883-3883. See you there!

Acknowledgment of Contribution

This letter acknowledges that a company has contributed to a charity.

JJT: HEAVY EQUIPMENT
1288 E. U.S. 63 • Sioux City, IA 50585

April 25, 199X

William J. Buchheit
President
Sanders and Thoms
348 Lincolnway Drive
South Sioux City, IA 50585

Dear Mr. Buchheit:

The United Benefit for Community Improvement would like to thank you and your employees for your generous contribution to this year's fund drive. Your contribution of $99,751 is the largest corporate/employee contribution so far.

Donna Truemper, your UBCI chairperson, will let the employees of Sanders and Thoms know of their accomplishment. This year they gave an average of 2.75% of their income to the fund. Their contribution and yours will definitely help us meet our goal of $2 million.

All of you at Sanders and Thoms are to be commended for your generosity. Thank you again for your contribution.

Sincerely yours,

Lannie Miller
Campaign Chairperson

LJM:wit

First Acknowledgment of the Contribution

General Statement About the Contribution

Specific Details

Second Acknowledgment

Acknowledgment of Accomplishment

This letter expresses goodwill and acknowledges an accomplishment by someone who has a relationship to the company (employee, relative of an employee, friend of the company).

KJZ, Inc.
45 Western Hills Rd., St. Paul, MN 55445

July 28, 199X

Jake Tillis
R.R. 1
Lake Woebegone, MN 56151

Dear Mr. Tillis:

Accomplishment

First Acknowledgment

KJZ is proud to have the new Twin Cities Corporate 10K Marathon winner on its staff. Your performance in Saturday's run was impressive.

General Statement About the Accomplishment

It was most thrilling to see you cross the finish line wearing your KJZ T-shirt and then watch the performance again on the evening news. Your hard work and training have paid off. The corporate trophy was the result of your accomplishment.

Second Acknowledgment

Thank You

The trophy will be prominently displayed in the front lobby at KJZ. Thank you for representing us so ably.

Sincerely,

Kevin J. Zimmerman
President

KJZ:rmz

Thank You

Similar to the letter expressing appreciation, this letter thanks an employee or business associate for something they have done.

King's Court Auto
1500 Wright Way, Kitty Hawk, NC 27831

November 17, 199X

Lee Kim Park
23 Timberline Dr.
Tarryton, NC 27789

Dear Mr. Park:

First Thank You

On behalf of the management at King's Court Auto, I would like to thank you for your recent participation in the United Way Campaign as Region 7's Unit Leader.

General Comments

Encouragement

Your leadership in United Way not only helps the community but also reflects well on King's Court Auto. Civic participation is important, and we are proud of our employees when they take part in the community.

Second Thank You

Thank you once again for all your hard work. Hats off to you!

Sincerely yours,

Donald King
Chairman of the Board

DSK:hey

Grant Request

Although most grant requests require a specific application form, you still need to send a cover letter with the form. This letter is a sample cover letter.

Salina Community College
45 Cottonwood Dr., Salina, KS 67401

October 14, 199X

Cassandra L. Meyerhoff
Director of Grants
Salina Area Grant Office
350 First Street
Salina, KS 67401

Dear Ms. Meyerhoff:

Request for Grant

We would like to request a $15,000 grant for Salina Community College to improve access for the handicapped. I have enclosed our grant application.

Requirements

Background Information and Summary of Need

The majority of the buildings on the Salina Community College campus were built prior to 1953. Those built after 1945 are accessible to the handicapped. Unfortunately, Atkinson Auditorium, where we hold graduation, monthly convocations and other major events, was built in 1932 and is not accessible to the handicapped. The $15,000 grant would allow us to install ramps at each entrance and remove a row of seats for wheelchairs, making the entire campus accessible to the handicapped.

Thank You

Thank you for your prompt action on this grant. We shall look forward to hearing from you.

Sincerely yours,

Mary Ellen Feldman
Director of Physical Facilities

MEF:klo

Invitation to Serve

This letter invites someone with the company to serve on a committee or in a position — governmental or charitable.

GREATER PITTSBURGH FAMILY FUND
760 Allegheny Dr., Mt. Lebanon, PA 16301

July 1, 199X

Lucinda M. Grimschaw
993 White Water Way
Mt. Lebanon, PA 16301

Dear Ms. Grimschaw:

Invitation

We of the Greater Pittsburgh Family Fund would like to invite you to chair the Health Committee for 199X.

Explanation

The Health Committee disburses funds to help families who have exhausted all other medical resources. We are asking you to chair this committee of eight people for one year.

Persuasion

Your leadership and organizational skills are essential for our continuing success. As a committee member last year, your dedication to health was apparent. Here is your chance to make a difference in the lives of families in desperate need. We need your combination of compassion and competence in directing the Health Committee.

Requirements and Duties

Presently, the committee meets weekly to review requests and act on them. Additionally, you would need to prepare a monthly disbursement report to be presented to the Greater Pittsburgh Family Fund's monthly Steering Committee. You would report directly to me.

Thank You
Set Deadline

Thank you for considering this offer. Please let me know by July 15, 199X, if you are able to take this position. I look forward to working with you.

Sincerely yours,

Coretta Marshall
General Chairperson

CAM:tpw

Membership Invitation

Membership drives are common in volunteer organizations. Here is how you can hook your reader and catch a member.

COMMUNITY VALORS
642 Rocky Mountain Road • Denver, CO 80023

September 14, 199X

Mary E. Marius
866 Aspen Place
Denver, CO 80025

Dear Ms. Marius:

Benefit

As a new resident of Denver, wouldn't you like to get to know the city and its people better? Then consider the service and networking opportunities Community Valors could provide you.

Background

We meet monthly to plan service projects that improve life in Denver. You have already seen our trademark red vests on the job at the blood bank where you so generously gave of yourself last Friday. We are always looking for enthusiastic and empathetic people to participate in our organization. We think you meet the qualifications!

Projects

Some of our projects this past year have included establishing a food and toiletry pantry for people with AIDS, tutoring for people whose second or third language is English, and emergency aid to people suffering from disaster, disease or distress.

Dues

Each project is funded by membership dues of $90 per year and special contributions from area businesses.

Invitation

Our annual membership drive began this week and runs through the end of September. We invite you to become part of the largest volunteer service organization in the state.

Ask for Permission to Contact

May we call upon you to answer any questions you may have about Community Valors and to encourage you to join our efforts? Please send the enclosed postcard to us now. We promise to serve your interests and find outlets for your talents in Community Valors.

Sincerely,

Mac Williams and Beth Tomasic
Membership Drive Co-chairs

Postscript Invitation

P.S. Save some time so you can begin sharing your time: Send your membership dues in with the postcard, and we'll get you into a project right away. We have a red vest waiting for you!

Refusal of a Request

This letter refuses a request made by another company or individual.

MARION MEDICAL SUPPLY
883 Union N.W. • Marion, KY 41503

November 16, 199X

M.D. Easton
Cranston County Democratic Chairman
995 Rapid Run Rd.
Marion, KY 41503

Dear Mr. Easton:

Refusal

I regret that I will be unable to run for County Commissioner as we discussed last Friday. It is flattering to be asked, but circumstances do not allow me to run for office at this time.

Reason

I am declining because of prior commitments to my family and my business. I would not have the time to campaign or to devote to the position because of the prolonged illness of my mother and the amount of travel required by my business. I shall continue to actively support the Democratic Party, both through volunteer efforts and monetary support.

Thank You for Understanding

Thank you for considering me. I appreciate your understanding.

Sincerely yours,

Duke Snow

DDS:van

Expressions of Appreciation

This letter expresses appreciation for an act by an employee or a business associate.

DEMOCRATIC COMMITTEE
995 Rapid Run Road • Marion, KY 41503

October 30, 199X

Duke Snow
Marion Medical Supply
883 Union N.W.
Marion, KY 41503

Dear Mr. Snow:

Express Appreciation

Thank you for your support in our recent election. Your hard work is greatly appreciated along with your monetary contributions.

General Statement About the Situation

When you indicated last November that you would not be able to run for commissioner, I was disappointed. But I knew that you would support us in any way possible. Once again, you came through. It was because of your untiring, behind-the-scenes work that we were able to sweep the election. You are essential to Cranston County Democrats.

Reiterate Appreciation

Thank you once again for all your hard work. Without you, we couldn't have done it.

Sincerely yours,

M.D. "Doc" Easton
Cranston County Democratic Chair

MDE:klw

Appointment to Office

This letter congratulates the recipient on his appointment to an office in government or a charitable organization.

"Public Office is a public trust."

— W.C. Hudson, Slogan for the 1884 Cleveland campaign

Clothier's International
793 W. Washington, Tanville, RI 02878

September 30, 199X

Samuel R. Grant
1515 Sycamore Lane
Tanville, RI 02878

Dear Sam:

Congratulations on your recent appointment to the Tanville City Council. You should be proud of your accomplishment.

Our policy of civic leave encourages our employees to participate in government. Your long-standing commitment to the community and this recent appointment make us proud to have you on our staff.

Keep up the good work. We need more people like you looking out for Tanville's interests.

Sincerely,

Lisa M. Mannerheim
Assistant Vice President

LMM:jjk

Congratulations

General Statement About Company

Specific Recognition

Encouragement (optional)

Appointment to a Committee

This letter congratulates an employee or business associate on an appointment to a committee.

Keystone Educational Agency
562 Rolling Hills • Birdsdale, PA 19508

January 10, 199X

Karen Gorman
Box 67, R.R. 4
New Jerusalem, PA 18825

Dear Karen:

First Congratulations

Congratulations on your appointment to the Excellence in Education Committee for Lucas County. We are pleased that one of our staff will be representing us and know that your experience and education will serve you well.

General Statement (optional)

Striving for excellence in education in the tri-state area is of utmost importance. You have worked hard in the past supporting educational issues, and I'm sure you will continue your strong leadership role in the Excellence in Education Committee for Lucas County.

Second Congratulations (optional)

If you need any help or resources, be sure to let us know. We are proud of your success and know that this appointment will bring you much personal satisfaction.

Sincerely,

Benjamin K. Douglas
Superintendent

BKD:ssp

Compliment

Similar to letters that congratulate and acknowledge accomplishments, this letter compliments someone (employee, relative of an employee, friend of the company) on something he or she has done.

KIDS WORLD
2255 Wilson Blvd., Galentine, IL 61036

January 20, 199X

C.K. Leister
R.R. 5
Galentine, IL 61036

Dear C.K.:

Your fine performance in the Galentine Community Theatre last Friday was noteworthy. You brought Stanley to life in *A Streetcar Named Desire.*

It is exciting for me to see fellow employees involved in the fine arts. I'm sure you are aware that Kids World has been a corporate supporter of the Galentine Community Theatre since its inception.

You are to be commended for your fine interpretation. Keep up the good work.

Sincerely,

Lorraine J. Black
President

LJB:kkc

First Compliment

Relate to the Company (optional)

Second Compliment (optional)

Invitation to Speak

This letter invites someone from the community to speak at a company-related function.

Enterprises, Ltd.
345 Waconia Rd., Denver, CO 80023

June 5, 199X

Leonard Takamoto
5699 Mission Highway
Bismarck, ND 58578

Dear Mr. Takamoto:

Invitation
Meeting Details

We of Enterprises, Ltd. would like to ask you to speak at our Annual Stockholders' Meeting, August 10, 199X, in Denver.

Explanation

Specific Topic

Your reputation as an entrepreneur in the field of small businesses interests us. As you may know, Enterprises, Ltd. acts as a clearing house for small businesses and supplies ideas and seed money for new small businesses. Your recent article in *Success* speaks to the topic that we would like our stockholders to hear: "The Future of America Lies in Its Small Businesses." We hope you will consider this offer.

Thank You
Attachment
Deadline for Reply
Contact Information

Thank you for your time. Attached is a sheet outlining all of the particulars: remuneration, schedules, hotel and airline arrangements. Please let me know by June 15 if you will accept this speaking engagement. You can reach me at 208-555-7793.

Sincerely yours,

Hal J. Martinson
Executive Administrative Assistant

HJM:lld

Complimenting a Speaker

This letter compliments a speaker who has spoken at a company-related function.

Enterprises, Ltd.
345 Waconia Rd., Denver, CO 80023

August 11, 199X

Leonard Takamoto
5699 Mission Highway
Bismarck, ND 58578

Dear Mr. Takamoto:

On behalf of the stockholders of Enterprises, Ltd., I would like to thank you for your speech yesterday. Several stockholders have called me this morning to say how much they agreed with what you were talking about.

I was particularly pleased to hear that Enterprises, Ltd. is right on target with our mission statement concerning small businesses. The renewal of a solid economic base in the rural areas of the Midwest is the result of forward-looking people such as yourself and our board of directors. Dr. Michael Pearson, one of our largest stockholders, spoke to me this morning and put it succinctly, "Mr. Takamoto hit the nail on the head when he pointed out that the future is in small businesses."

Please send me your expense report for immediate reimbursement. Include copies of receipts and an invoice number to facilitate this transaction.

Thank you for your inspiring speech. It was our privilege to hear you.

Sincerely yours,

Calvin R. Stiers
President

CRS:est

First Compliment

Elaboration (optional)

Testimony

Thank You
Second Compliment

Letter to Legislator Showing Support

This letter shows support of a bill being considered. The elaboration paragraph builds the writer's credibility and increases the power of the support.

Mario's Pasta Inns, Inc.
803 King Ave., Odessa, TX 76514

September 8, 199X

The Honorable Sarah Williams
Representative
Government Offices
9900 Ralston Way
Austin, TX 78603

Dear Ms. Williams:

Statement of Support

Your continued concern for both restaurant owners and customers is admirable and H.R. 305 demonstrates that concern. I support H.R. 305 that you recently introduced.

Elaboration (optional)

I own Mario's Pasta Inns, Inc., a chain of 15 Italian restaurants throughout Texas. Additionally, I am the past spokesperson for Restaurateurs International and am an active member of its governing board. We wholeheartedly support your bill that limits the sales tax on meals eaten out. We can see that raising the tax will hurt the owners and our customers.

Thank You

Thank you for your concern and your untiring pursuit of keeping taxes in line. You have our support.

Sincerely yours,

Mario Napoli
President

MDN:klu

Letter to Legislator Showing Concern

This letter shows concern over a bill being considered. Although elaboration is still optional in the second paragraph, it builds credibility for the writer's opinion and offers a persuasive comparison. This paragraph cannot be discounted easily.

Mario's Pasta Inns, Inc.
803 King Ave., Odessa, TX 76514

September 8, 199X

The Honorable Hank Schlesselman
Representative
Government Offices
9900 Ralston Way
Austin, TX 78603

Dear Mr. Schlesselman:

Statement of Concern

I am most concerned about your support for H.R. 376. Its stringent restaurant sanitation requirements will double our costs, which will, of course, be passed on to the customer. This may put many restaurants out of business.

Elaboration (optional)

I own Mario's Pasta Inns, Inc., a chain of 15 Italian restaurants throughout Texas. Additionally, I am the past spokesperson for Restaurateurs International and am an active member of its governing board. Our organization has thoroughly researched sanitation laws for restaurants throughout the world. Texas currently has the most stringent laws, and is recognized as a leader in the area of sanitation for restaurants. H.R. 376 in all cases has standards that even our medical labs would have trouble meeting.

Restate Concern

I hope you will seriously consider the impact H.R. 376 would have on our economy. Such a bill can only cause the loss of jobs and income and create disgruntled customers. Please withdraw your support of H.R. 376.

Sincerely yours,

Mario Napoli
President

MDN:klu

Checklist

☐ Did you state the purpose of the letter in the first part?

Chapter 8 — Personal Business Letters

8

There are times when you write on behalf of yourself rather than for the entire company. This chapter includes samples to help you write personal business letters. The broad categories are as follows:

At the side of the page, you will find a brief explanation of each part of the letter. The first letter, on page 97, identifies each section of the letter. Subsequent letters identify only changes to the basic format.

Writing Personal Business Letters

Step-by-Step Guide

These letters are similar to goodwill letters. They are letters in which you promote goodwill toward your employees, their relatives and business associates.

Step 1: The first part of the letter states your purpose. Depending on the reason for writing the letter, this may vary from congratulating a business associate or employee to extending a holiday greeting.

Step 2: The second part of the letter gives the details or background information for the first part. This may include details about an employee's accomplishments or personal comments concerning the first part.

Step 3: The last part of the letter acts as a summary, reminding the recipient of the general nature of the letter. It may include deadlines, a thank-you note or a re-request. It is not necessary in many of the personal business letters to have a third part.

Note: At the end of this chapter is a checklist to use when you write a personal business letter.

Congratulations

Congratulate an employee, relative of an employee or business associate on an accomplishment.

Wilson and Company **1515 W. 23rd Avenue • Tulsa, OK 74103**	**Letterhead**
August 13, 199X	**Date**
Tim Ryan 3469 Campbell St. Tulsa, OK 74103	**Inside Address**
Dear Tim:	**Salutation**
Congratulations on your win in the Junior Division at the Tulsa Rodeo.	**Congratulations**
To be able to win at such a young age is quite an accomplishment. I understand that not only did you win the Junior Division hands down, but also came within points of the Senior Division winner.	**Personal Comments** (optional)
Your mom is so proud of you. Congratulations once again!	**Second Congratulations** (optional)
Sincerely,	**Complimentary Close**
Karen R. Detweiler President	**Signature**
KRD:cro	**Additional Information**

Congratulations

This letter congratulates an employee, relative of an employee or friend of the company.

LINDER AIRPLANES
515 Airport Road, Waterloo, IA 50707

August 6, 199X

Tommy Determan
Highway 20
Dunkerton, IA 50626

Dear Tommy:

First Congratulations

Congratulations on winning the soap box derby during "My Waterloo Days." Your father couldn't stop talking about how proud he was of your victory.

Personal Comments (optional)

I was interested in your win because I, too, was a soap box derby winner 21 years ago in Akron, Ohio. There's nothing quite like the thrill of knowing that something you've made is capable of winning.

Second Congratulations (optional)

Congratulations once again and good luck at the Nationals!

Sincerely,

Charles M. Norris
President

CMN:cro

Birthday Wishes

This brief letter wishes someone (employee, relative of an employee, friend of the company, business associate) a happy birthday.

"It has long been an axiom of mine that the little things are infinitely most important."

— Sherlock Holmes

Oglethorpe's and Osman
619 Leisure Blvd.
Watchatee, FL 33873

May 25, 199X

King Montgomery
774 Rising Hill Rd.
Lakeland, FL 32340

Dear King:

Is it that time of year again? Where has the time gone? Hope your birthday is a happy one. We appreciate your work here at Oglethorpe's and Osman and hope that we enjoy many more birthdays together.

Sincerely,

Lawrence Oglethorpe
President

LJO:ccy

Birthday Wishes

Holiday Greetings

This short letter wishes an employee or business associate holiday greetings. This is particularly useful for those employees or business associates whose religion is not covered by the standard business greeting cards.

Goodwill Greeting

GIBRALTER GEMS
112 Appian Way
Teasdale, WV 26656

December 15, 199X

Joshua Schwartz
38 Fairview Ct.
Teasdale, WV 26656

Dear Josh:

The warmest of holiday greetings to you and your family. We at Gibralter Gems hope this holiday season brings you the best of everything. Our regards to all of you.

Sincerely,

Thomas "Tip" Gibralter

TJG:ald

Birth of a Child

This letter congratulates the recipient on the birth of a child.

CHINA DOLLS FOR YOU
400 E. 60th St., Reno, NV 89502

June 4, 199X

Lorraine R. Morris
55 Willow Bend Ct., #776
Reno, NV 89501

Dear Lorraine:

There is nothing more exciting than a new baby. You and T.K. must be proud. We were all thrilled to hear about Travis' birth and know you are, too.

First Congratulations

All of us are looking forward to seeing you, T.K. and Travis when you come to visit us next week. That's the time for our traditional "Shower of Gifts."

General Statement

Congratulations, Lorraine! We're all envious of your new little one. Take care of all three of you.

Second Congratulations (optional)
Goodwill

Sincerely,

Shelli McAdam
Office Manager

SAM:kad

Marriage

"Marriages are made in heaven, and consummated on Earth."
— John Lyly

This letter extends congratulations or best wishes when an employee or business associate gets married.

Smith, Jones and Yanacek
Counselors at Law
231 1st St. S.E., Remington, MO 63302

February 22, 199X

Linda Gleason
572 Westwood, Apartment B
Remington, MO 63302

Dear Linda:

First Congratulations

On behalf of Smith, Jones and Yanacek, I would like to extend our best wishes on your marriage to Terry Gleason. We all wish you the happiest of times.

Personal Comment

It is always a pleasure to share in the happiness of one of our employees. In your case, it was even more so, because you have been such an important part of our firm. I know I speak for all of us when I say that it couldn't have happened to a nicer person. We all look forward to your return after your honeymoon and hope that we will meet Terry soon.

Second Congratulations (optional)

Best wishes once again. We'll see you in a couple of weeks.

Sincerely,

Montgomery Smith
Senior Partner

MGS:gab

Illness — Hospital

This letter offers sympathy for an employee who is hospitalized.

FT. DODGE FURNACES
445 Grand Ave.
Ft. Dodge, IA 50501

January 10, 199X

Carl Mattus-Wilson
319 Main
Manson, IA 50563

Dear Carl:

I am sorry to hear that you have been hospitalized. I'm sure that the staff at Trinity General will take good care of you and get you on your way. Please call us if you have any questions regarding the company's health insurance.

Ft. Dodge Furnaces relies heavily on its employees and will feel your absence. I hope that you will recover quickly. We look forward to your return.

Sincerely,

Ole Munson
President

OHM:ijd

Sympathy
Goodwill
Assistance

Additional Comments

Thank You

This letter thanks someone (employee, relative of an employee, business associate) for something that was done.

Wobbly Horse Gift Shop
4866 Kilimanjaro Dr., Ann Arbor, MI 48897

April 3, 199X

Robert Wu
300 Lister Ln.
Ann Arbor, MI 48898

Dear Mr. Wu:

First Thank You

I want to thank you for sending me the address and phone number of the gift shop in Hong Kong.

Explanation (optional)

I called them this evening to ask about the tablecloths you told me about. You were right. They were most cordial and reasonable in their prices. I was able to order 10 tablecloths at a fraction of what they would have cost here in the States.

Second Thank You

Thank you once again for your kind gesture.

Sincerely,

R. James Robinson

RJR:klr

Apology

This is a formal apology. Such letters usually deal with social events.

Trundle, Trundle and Smith
P.O. Box 2290, Frost, AZ 85603

December 1, 199X

Warren and Marie Lambertson
4610 Country Club Way
Frost, AZ 85603

Dear Mr. and Mrs. Lambertson:

Please accept my apologies for missing your Thanksgiving brunch on November 23. I hope my last-minute change of plans did not inconvenience you too much.

As you know, I had planned on attending and was looking forward to it. However, my brother, who lives in Boston, Georgia, had emergency bypass surgery, and his wife asked me to be with her. Had that not happened, naturally I would have been with you.

Once again, I ask for your understanding in this matter and hope that my frantic, last-minute call to bow out was acceptable.

Sincerely yours,

Thomas J. Trundle, Sr.

TJT:mal

First Apology

Explanation and Personal Comments (optional)

Second Apology (optional)

Inquiries

This letter asks for information to be used by the company.

Cat Man Dew Pet Suppliers
853 Regal Ave., Oklahoma City, OK 73009

February 14, 199X

Pekka H. Huovienin
34 Raamintinuu
58 Helsinki 00580
Finland

Dear Mr. Huovienin:

Inquiry
Compliment

We are trying to locate information on a breed of cat called the Suomi Shorthair and understand that you are the leading expert on cats in Finland.

Explanation

We have a client who is interested in buying a Suomi Shorthair. She had seen one once at the New York Feline Show but has been unable to locate one since. She came to our shop and requested that we help her. Since the breed originated in Finland, we thought you might be able to give us some more information. We are most interested in the names of breeders that may have kittens for sale.

Thank You
Contact Information

We will call you within the next month to follow up on this inquiry. Thank you for all your trouble. We look forward to talking to you.

Sincerely,

Kathleen "Cat" Pence

KMP:nip

Request

This letter requests an individual or company to act on the request.

PDQ Truckers
P.O. Box 2068, Denver, CO 80393-2068

August 21, 199X

Cameron Mrstik
Mrstik's Mobile Station
582 Robinwood
Minihaha, MN 55437

Dear Mr. Mrstik:

Request

Would you please return the black leather jacket that was left in your gas station last Saturday?

Explanation

One of our truckers, Sam MacIntyre, left his leather jacket when he was on a run for us. Another of our truckers mentioned to Sam that he thought he saw a jacket just like Sam's hanging on your wall. He said it had to be Sam's; there are few leather jackets that say, "Ivydale, West Virginia," on them. Sam asked us to call you as he's on vacation in the Bahamas. We have tried repeatedly to reach you by phone, but your phone is always busy.

Specific Information

Thank You

Please send the jacket as soon as possible, C.O.D. Thank you for your prompt response.

Sincerely,

Patrick D. Quentin
President

PDQ:msq

Refusal

This letter is an answer to the request letter and gives the reasons why the recipient won't act on the writer's request.

Mrstik's Mobile Station
582 Robinwood, Minihaha, MN 55437

August 25, 199X

Patrick D. Quentin, President
PDQ Truckers
P.O. Box 2068
Denver, CO 80393-2068

Dear Mr. Quentin:

Refusal

I would like to return Mr. MacIntyre's jacket to him, but I don't have it.

Explanation

The jacket your trucker saw says, "I love Dale, Wes and Virginia." I had that jacket made specially for my wife. Those are our three children's names. I checked our register of truckers and there was no Sam MacIntyre at our station on the Saturday you mentioned.

Added Service

Perhaps he was at Mrs. Rick's Mobile Station on the interstate. The phone number there is (612) 499-3827. People get us mixed up all the time.

Regret Goodwill

I'm sorry I couldn't help you. I hope Mr. MacIntyre finds his jacket soon.

Sincerely,

Cameron Mrstik

CJM:mjm

Checklist

- ☐ Is the tone of the letter sincere?
- ☐ Did you state the purpose of the letter in the first part?
- ☐ Did you give background information or details in the second part?
- ☐ If you used a third part, did you recongratulate, thank or set deadlines for your request?

Chapter 9 — Letters of Condolence

Here are samples to help you write the most difficult of all letters to compose, condolence letters. The broad categories are as follows:

At the side of the page you will find a brief explanation of each part of the letter. The first letter, on page 113, identifies each section of the letter. Subsequent letters identify only changes to the basic format.

Writing Letters of Condolence

Step-by-Step Guide

Although sympathy cards are available, a letter of condolence is more personal. Letters of condolence should be written with a sincere tone. If at all possible, reflect on the person who has died.

Step 1: The first part of the letter offers your condolences.

Step 2: The second part of the letter, if possible, should reflect on the person who has died. If you knew the person well, personal recollections are appropriate. If you did not know the person well or at all, this part is optional; although if you can relate this person's life to your own in some way, you should include this part.

Step 3: The last part of the letter offers further condolences or support.

Note: At the end of this chapter is a checklist to use when you write a condolence letter.

On the Death of a Business Associate

GRAHAM'S **573 Westdale Road • Santa Fe, NM 87505**	Letterhead
October 6, 199X	Date
Lou Gosnell, President Richman's Realty 908 Winky Santa Fe, NM 87505	Inside Address
Dear Lou:	Salutation
I was shocked to hear of the death of your partner, Max Wassermann. Although I knew he was ill, I was still taken by surprise by his sudden passing.	Condolences
Max and I worked together at the old Cramer's Store in downtown Santa Fe when we first arrived here in 1934. I will never forget his immense capacity for helping other people. I share your sorrow at this time.	Personal Recollection of Deceased
If there is any way that I can help, please let me know. Rest assured that your loss is all of Santa Fe's loss.	Further Condolences or Offers of Support
Sincerely,	Complimentary Close
Geo. "Pinky" Graham	Signature
GGG:sok	Additional Information

Writing Letters of Condolence

On the Death of Mother

TRAINS UNLIMITED
209 Grant
Quincy, IL 62321

December 11, 199X

Marilyn Lockwood
542 Maine
Quincy, IL 62322

Dear Marilyn:

Condolences

Please let me extend my deepest sympathy on behalf of all the staff here at Trains Unlimited on the passing of your mother.

Personal Recollection of Deceased (optional)

I know that you spoke many times of how difficult your mother's battle with cancer was. I'm sure that, though we are saddened by her death, we share your relief that she is now at peace. She was a brave woman.

Further Condolences or Offers of Support

Please accept our sympathy. We have taken up a collection for a memorial contribution and sent it to the American Cancer Society in your mother's name.

Sincerely,

Gloria Williams
Vice President, Sales

GAW:vab

On the Death of Father

Lindlemeier's Tree Farms
R.R. 2 • Marlboro, VT 00192

November 1, 199X

Truk Pham
Box 33
Windham, VT 00200

Dear Truk:

I was saddened to hear that your father died last Friday and wish to extend my sympathy.

Although I did not know your father well, I did have a chance to meet him on a couple of occasions. He was proud of his new country and of being able to help his children become established here in the United States. Though his loss is painful, you have much to be proud of with your father.

If there is some way that Tilly and I can help you and your family, let us know. Please take as much time from work as you need to get your father's affairs in order.

Sincerely,

Jake and Tilly Lindlemeier

JEL:mfp

Condolences

Personal Recollection of Deceased (optional)

Further Condolences or Offers of Support

On the Death of Wife

Berryhill's Furniture Mart
4455 Southdale Plaza • Portland, OR 97276

March 1, 199X

Charles M. Potter, Sr.
77 Sunnyset
Portland, OR 97273

Dear Charles:

Condolences

Please accept our condolences on the untimely passing of your wife, Lydia. It is difficult to understand why such tragedies happen, and I do not understand why Lydia was taken from you so early in your life together.

Personal Recollection of Deceased (optional)

You must now surround yourself with good friends and the pleasant memories you have of Lydia. I remember her beaming smile at the company picnics. She seemed to have a zest for life that few of us do and was willing to share that zest with others. I shall never forget her enthusiastic win of the sack race last year.

Further Condolences Offers of Support

Please accept what little comfort these words can give you. If we can help you in any way, please call.

Sincerely,

N.K. Berryhill

NKB:pmc

On the Death of Husband

THOMPSON'S JANITORIAL SERVICE
4410 Rodney Drive • Armada, AL 35739

July 17, 199X

Ida Louise Trotter
555 Keanhorn Split
Jackstown, AL 36265

Dear Mrs. Trotter:

Our deepest sympathy to you and your family on the death of your husband, Ned. He was a dear friend to so many of us here at Thompson's.

When Ned first came to Thompson's, he told us that he was here to stay and stay he did — 35 years. I am happy that he enjoyed a few years of his retirement before he became ill.

We at Thompson's are here when you need us. Please accept this token as a memorial for Ned.

Sincerely,

George Ray Thompson

GRT:sse

Condolences

Personal Recollection of Deceased (optional)

Further Condolences Offers of Support

On the Death of a Child

KFPJ–FM 89.4
212 Kalispell Rd., Butte, MT 59732

February 23, 199X

Jean and Ike Nelson
R.R. 3
Flying Horn Ranch
Butte, MT 59732

Dear Mr. and Mrs. Nelson:

Condolences

I was shocked to hear of the death of your son, Bobby. Such losses defy understanding.

Personal Recollection of Deceased (optional)

Bobby used to come in on Saturday with Ike to the station and listen to me do my show. He was forever wanting me to play John Denver's "Rocky Mountain High." He said it made him feel good. I'll dedicate it to him this Saturday.

Further Condolences Offers of Support

If I can do anything to help, call. Ike, I'll cover for you as long as you need. God bless.

Sincerely,

Rocky Hopkins

RKH:ilb

On the Death of a Brother

TeleCommunications
239 Tandyview Ct., Arlington, TX 76126

May 12, 199X

Karen Swanson
7748 Irving Rd., Apartment #354
Arlington, TX 76216

Dear Karen:

I would like to offer my sympathy to you and your family on the passing of your brother.

Although I never met him, I feel as if I know him from all you've said about him at work. I'm sure his wife and children are pleased to know that you spoke so highly of him and his work with mentally retarded children. It is a shame that one so gifted must succumb so early in life.

If you need someone to talk to when you come back, I'll be here.

Sincerely,

Wanda Ferguson
Divisional Manager, TeleMarketing

WAF:bnr

Condolences

Personal Recollection of Deceased (optional)

Further Condolences Offers of Support

On the Death of a Sister

MODERN HEALTH INSURANCE COMPANY
909 Blackman Blvd.
Hartford, CT 06037

January 4, 199X

Rita Iverson
2020 Blue Jay
E. Hartford, CT 06087

Dear Rita:

Condolences

I am most sorry to hear that your sister passed away from kidney failure last week.

Personal Recollection of Deceased (optional)

Linda Jean was a joy to work with the two years she was here at Modern Health. She always had such outrageous stories to tell. You can be thankful that she enjoyed life while she could.

Further Condolences
Offers of Support

Please offer my sympathy to your family, especially your mother. I'll take care of your mail while you are gone.

Sincerely,

Terry Glandon
Vice President, Claims

TAG:ccn

Checklist

- ☐ Is the letter sincere?
- ☐ Does the first part of the letter offer condolences?
- ☐ Does the second part of the letter include personal recollections if you knew the deceased?
- ☐ Does the third part of the letter offer further condolences and support?
- ☐ Does the letter comfort the bereaved?

Chapter 10—Letters About Employment Changes

10

One of the most demanding writing tasks is searching for a new position or hiring a new employee. Those are the two main categories of this chapter. Topics include the following employee responses:

Topics also include the following employer responses:

Writing Letters About Employment Changes

Step-by-Step Guide

Letters hiring employees are used by many companies in lieu of a contract drawn up by an attorney and are recognized as legal documents in many courts of law. It is therefore extremely important that you specify each aspect of employment for the prospective employee. Letters in this section also include samples of rejection letters and letters requesting confidential information.

Step 1: The first part of the letter states your purpose. This may be anything from offering a position to requesting information.

Step 2: The second part of the letter gives the details or background information of the first part. If you are offering a position, it is appropriate in this section to give all of the details concerning the position. If you are requesting information, you should explain why you need the information. If you are rejecting an application, you should provide a reason for the rejection. If you are recommending or providing a reference for someone, state specific knowledge, skills and abilities the person has that will benefit the reader.

Step 3: The last part of the letter acts as a summary reminding the recipient of the general nature of the letter. This part clarifies the action that must be taken, if any.

Note: At the end of this chapter is a checklist to use when you write letters to hire employees.

Reference Request

Asking a person to be a reference is awkward for most people. This letter will help with that task.

Cody Helm
One Tailgate Dr.
Sioux City, IA 50584

December 2, 199X — **Date**

Jason Tompkins, Jr.
JJT: Heavy Equipment
1288 E. U.S. 63
Sioux City, IA 50585 — **Inside Address**

Dear Jason: — **Salutation**

Request Details

May I use your name as a reference for a job I hope to get? I am applying for risk manager openings at Johns Oil Company, Fast Food Inc., and Ploish Publishing. Our experience together at JJT helped give me the confidence to try for these jobs.

Update

Since I graduated with an Associate Degree in Risk Management last spring, I have taken several courses in industrial engineering. I am experienced with OSHA regulations and a variety of plant operational systems.

Personal Note

Being both co-workers and friends for many years, I naturally thought of you as a reference. If you are comfortable with that idea, please return the enclosed self-addressed stamped postcard to me stating your approval. I'd appreciate your help, of course, but also understand not wanting strangers calling any time wanting inside information about someone who out-fishes you on every camping trip. Yet, I know I could have a great career with any of these companies and could then afford to treat you to a fish dinner at a fine restaurant!

Thank You

Thanks either way for being a friend — and the son of a heavy equipment company owner who hired a poor fisherman years back!

Sincerely, — **Complimentary Close**

Cody — **Closing**

Waiver of Confidentiality

This letter is a form signed by an employee giving the employer permission to provide information to parties such as welfare agencies or spouses who request it. This protects the employer from a lawsuit for invasion of privacy.

Wholesome Eggs, Inc.
R.R. 3
Bandville, AL 35542

Acknowledgment

I, the undersigned, acknowledge that my employer has received a request from Crystal Ziesser for information concerning my employment.

Permission Given

I grant my employer full permission to provide the information described as salary history, benefit history and sick leave accrued.

Signature

Employee

Date

Sept. 5, 199X
Date

Request for Meeting

Asking for a meeting or an interview is an essential job skill. Here is how to do it.

456 El Camino
Santa Fe, NM 87501

April 25, 199X

Maggie Montoya
Escrow Department
Valley National Bank
P.O. Box 99
Espanola, NM 87532

Dear Ms. Montoya:

Thank you for your response to my April 19, 199X, inquiry concerning the position of escrow representative at Valley National Bank.

If you have any time available on either May 7 or 8, I would appreciate ten minutes of your day to review a five-step plan for developing an escrow division in one month. This plan could benefit the entire bank. If the plan interests you, we could then schedule additional time to discuss how I might assist VNB in achieving its escrow goals.

I will call on May 2 to arrange an appointment. I look forward to meeting you in person.

Sincerely,

Carrie Gonzales

Thank You
Reference
Position

Request

Benefit

Contact Information

Interview Confirmation

Keeping your name in front of a potential employer is an effective way of persuading someone to hire you. Confirming an interview achieves that purpose while reducing confusion regarding appointment details.

456 El Camino
Santa Fe, NM 87501

May 1, 199X

Maggie Montoya
Escrow Department
Valley National Bank
P.O. Box 99
Espanola, NM 87532

Dear Ms. Montoya:

Thank You Confirmation

Thank you for making time in your schedule to see me on Monday, May 7, at 9:10 a.m.

Agenda and Intent

Although I will be brief in my presentation of the five steps to develop an escrow division, I will also be available to address any concerns you may have regarding the achievement of this goal within a month by your escrow staff.

Sincerely,

Carrie Gonzales

Thanks for Interview

Again, keep your name on a potential employer's desk and in his or her mind. Demonstrating manners is a persuasive tool for obtaining a job, too.

456 El Camino
Santa Fe, NM 87501

May 7, 199X

Maggie Montoya
Escrow Department
Valley National Bank
P.O. Box 99
Espanola, NM 87532

Dear Ms. Montoya:

Thank you for the interview today. Your joke about the lonesome lawyer still makes me laugh.

I appreciate your consideration of my qualifications and application for the job of escrow representative. I will check in with you next Monday to see if you have made a decision about the position. If I may answer any questions or concerns, please call me at 982-6678, mornings.

Thank you again for your interest.

Sincerely,

Carrie Gonzales

Thank You Reminder

Contact Information

Thank You

Unsolicited Application

This letter may double as a cover letter for a resumé. The key descriptors are linked directly to the resumé material.

67 No. Hampshire Road
Redmond, WA 98052

October 12, 199X

Carver, Barrington & Stephens Imports
2345 Brown Ave.
Seattle, WA 98104

Dear Mr. Carver:

Purpose
Position
Reference

I am responding to the in-house posting for the position of Associate Project Manager with your organization. A former colleague, Terry Barrington, alerted me to the opening and suggested that I contact you directly.

Background
Benefit

I have four years of experience with Michaels & Wade in Redmond, where I specialized in Management Information Systems. As you update your computer network and applications, you will need expertise in every department of your import business. The key descriptors below highlight areas of my experience and education that you will find most pertinent.

Specific Skills

Computer Skills: DOS, WordPerfect, Lotus, Harvard Graphics; Associate's Degree in Computer Science, 1993.

Communication Skills: Excellent grammar and usage in writing; good oral presentation and training skills; wrote and delivered annual department report for board of directors.

Sales Experience: Retail sales associate as high school and college student for three years at Pier Trading Post.

Supervisory Experience: Assistant to the associate warehouse supervisor at Michaels & Wade for four years.

Request
Contact Information
Availability

May I arrange a time to meet with you or your agent early next week? I will call your office on Thursday, October 16. I would be available immediately, just in time for the holiday rush at Carver, Barrington & Stephens Imports. My daytime phone number is 324-7889. Please call collect if you have questions.

Sincerely,

Charlie Lamble

Solicited Application

Although the employer initiates contact in this situation, the job seeker must respond with a personal sales pitch such as this sample letter.

77 Longmeadow Ave.
Tulsa, OK 74135

August 3, 199X

David Fronte, Vice President
Professional Chemical Institute
864 Manhattan
Pittsburg, KS 66762

Dear Mr. Fronte:

Thank you for your telephone call this morning requesting my application for product developer. I am pleased that our friend, Kelly Greene, spoke so highly of me.

Your call came at an opportune time in my career. I am encouraged that your company's direction may be the very avenue I have sought for several new product ideas. Your goal of a 10-percent increase in products during the next two years is a challenge I am ready to accept.

I am eager to discuss this potential growth with you next Wednesday in your office at 2:15 p.m. as you suggested in our conversation today. In the meantime, please call me at 643-9975 should you need additional information prior to our meeting.

Thank you again for your interest.

Sincerely,

Brad Reed

Reminder
Position
Reference

Benefit

Confirmation
Contact Information

Thank You

Job Acceptance

Put this in writing! Confirm the specifications as you understand them.

One Tailgate Dr.
Sioux City, IA 50584

December 15, 199X

Mr. Kevin Johns
Johns Oil Company
R.R. Box 45
Sioux City, IA 50523

Dear Mr. Johns:

Acceptance
Date

It is a pleasure to accept the position of risk manager, effective January 3, 199X. I am eager to begin my new assignment.

Thank You
Intent

Thank you for your confidence in me. I will do my best to surpass the challenge presented by Johns Oil Company's phenomenal growth.

Sincerely,

Cody Helm

Job Rejection

This situation is difficult. If you know the job is a mismatch for your skills, be honest and then act to remedy the situation. Your integrity and credibility will expand with this letter.

174 Bittersweet St.
Broken Arrow, OK 74012

January 18, 199X

Carroll Connell, Director
Intercomp, Inc.
P. O. Box 23659
Tulsa, OK 74133

Dear Ms. Connell:

The position of executive drafting assistant sounds exciting. Thank you for considering me. However, I cannot accept this offer in good conscience at this time.

Position / Thank You / Rejection

The computer expertise this position requires for success demands more experience than I currently have. I want to do an excellent job; therefore, I am enrolling in a CAD course at Tulsa University. In four months I will have the experience to pursue a similar position with determination.

Reason

Decision

Perhaps TU instructors can suggest names of recent students who are prepared now to accept the responsibilities of the job. Someone better trained than I is waiting to discover Intercomp.

Suggestion for Alternative

Thank you again for thinking of me. It has been the incentive I needed to get the extra training I must have to continue in the drafting field. I intend to be prepared for the next executive drafting assistant opening as your company continues to expand its operation.

Thank You / Intent

Sincerely,

Chris Jensen

Positive Resignation

When you must "move on" to accept new opportunities, use this sample to guide the draft of your resignation.

Thomas Provost
34458 Seminole Lane
Tampa, FL 33640

February 2, 199X

Jerry Sanderstein
Sanderstein Aviation
8865 Hidden River Parkway
Tampa, FL 33637

Dear Jerry:

Feelings / Resignation / Date / Reason

With deep regret and with some excitement, I must resign as night shift supervisor, effective March 1, 199X. My family will be relocating to Georgia this spring so my wife can pursue a lucrative offer in a law firm. This is an opportunity we cannot overlook.

Assistance Offer

I will be glad to assist in the training of my replacement. Our night shift has a couple of competent workers who would make excellent shift supervisors.

Thank You / Personal Note

Your encouragement during the past nine years has allowed me to grow in my responsibilities and capabilities. Thank you for these successful years. I will miss you, Jerry, as well as all my friends at Sanderstein Aviation. Your leadership provides me many fond memories. I wish you continued success.

Sincerely,

Tom

Negative Resignation

When you must leave a position under duress or stress, keep your explanation short, honest and positive. Despite your differences, you may need a reference from this employer in the future.

Julie Mast
345 Cedar Lake Road
Minneapolis, MN 55426

July 14, 199X

Leslie Young, Marketing Director
Marketing Towers
60 S. Ninth St.
Minneapolis, MN 55402

Dear Ms. Young:

I am resigning my position as special accounts representative, effective July 30, 199X.

Recent circumstances, incompatible with my personal values, require that I change my employment.

Thank you for the chance to work and learn at Marketing Towers.

Sincerely,

Julie Mast

Resignation Date

Reason

Thank You

Request for Employment Reference

This letter is from a company requesting a reference from a job applicant's previous employer.

TicToc Clocks, Inc.
8071 Speedway • Indianapolis, IN 46107

February 28, 199X

J. Carson Jamison, President
Weatherman Time
33 Little House Road
Columbus, OH 43230

Dear Mr. Jamison:

Statement of Candidate

We recently received an application from Carl Olson for the position of master carpenter with our firm. We understand he was previously employed by you.

Explanation of Request

We would appreciate any information you could give us concerning Mr. Olson's work habits, expertise as master carpenter and attitude. We would also appreciate your sharing with us the reason he no longer works for your firm.

Deadline Thank You

We look forward to hearing from you in early March. Please advise us if the information you provide is confidential. Thank you for your time in answering this request.

Sincerely,

James Vries
President

JBV:llo

Reference for Former Employee

This letter is a reference for a former employee who is seeking employment elsewhere.

Grant Middle School
901 Third St. • Columbia, OH 43230

March 12, 199X

Wendell R. Rathbourne, Principal
Jasper Heights Middle School
444 Calbryne Road
Shaker Heights, OH 44139

Dear Mr. Rathbourne:

Pauline O'Malley was employed as a teacher associate at Grant Middle School from April, 1988 to June, 1988. She was terminated because of a decrease in funding for special education.

During Ms. O'Malley's brief tenure she performed her duties very well. She was a teacher associate for eighth grade behavioral disorders classes and was well liked by both students and staff. The teachers she worked with speak highly of her abilities and willingness to cooperate.

I recommend Ms. O'Malley for any teacher associate position. Please feel free to call me or Marian Thompson, her past supervisor, for further information.

Sincerely,

Lillian M. Detterding
Principal

LMD:gan

Statement of Previous Employment

Explanation of Performance

Recommendation

Contact Information

Letter of Introduction

This letter introduces a person to a company or individual. Letters of introduction are similar to references, quite often describing the qualifications of the person to be introduced.

Campbell, Wilson and Sons
472 Captain's Drive — Boston, MA 02031

October 7, 199X

R. Hunter Wing
333 B. Ave., E.
Lincoln, NE 68530

Dear R.H.:

Introduction **Request**

I would like to introduce James N. Glandorf, who will be moving to Lincoln in November. As a fellow Pi Kappa Kappa, would you consider him for a position with your firm?

Background of Person Introduced and Relationship to the Writer

Mr. Glandorf worked in our law office during this last year. He was given the assignment of divorce cases, which he handled extremely well and was well on his way to establishing himself as one of the best divorce lawyers I have ever seen. James was in line for a partnership here also but wanted to return to his native Nebraska, which I understand, being a Midwesterner myself. I have enclosed a reference from each of our partners. I'm sure you'll find that all of us held James in the highest regard.

Request Clarification

Please take time to read the references and extend our greetings to James when he arrives. I have promised him nothing, but am sure that you will help him in any way that you would any other fellow Pi Kappa Kappa.

Sincerely,

George R. Campbell
Senior Partner

GRC:lpw
Enc. (4)

Letter of Recommendation

Letters of recommendation emphasize how a person worked on a previous job and his expertise. They should also include the relationship between the one seeking the job and the person writing the recommendation

GRANT WOOD HIGH SCHOOL
319 30th St. S.E. • Cedar Rapids, IA 52403

January 16, 199X

Linda A. Hagerman, Principal
Thomas Jefferson High School
788 Muscatine Ave.
Iowa City, IA 52240

Dear Ms. Hagerman:

It is with great pleasure that I recommend Mary Alice Westerly for the physics position at Thomas Jefferson.

Mrs. Westerly taught at Grant Wood High School from 1978 to 1986, during which time I was Principal. Her primary teaching responsibilities were physics, chemistry and ninth-grade general science. She was one of the best teachers we have ever had in the area of science, and we were deeply saddened when she and her family moved to Augusta, Maine. I can assure you that if I had a teaching position open in science, I would hire her. She is creative, deeply conscientious, professional and hard-working.

I strongly recommend her and am sure you will be more than satisfied with her performance in the classroom.

Sincerely,

Tom Maxwell
Principal

TJM:mer

Introduction

Relationship to the Writer
Background Information
Attributes of Person Recommended

Recommendation

Character Reference

Similar to the letter of recommendation, the character reference refers only to the character of the person. You should include your relationship with the person and how long you have known him or her.

St. John's-by-the-Lake Episcopal Church
298 Lakeshore Drive • Brandenburg, MN 56315

May 29, 199X

Klosterman Employment Agency
22 Linden Blvd.
Brandenburg, MN 56315

Dear Sir or Madam:

Introduction

I am most pleased to write a character reference for JoAnn Osterson.

Relationship to the Writer
Background Information
Attributes of Person Recommended

I have known JoAnn since I first moved to Brandenburg, when she was three years old. As rector of St. John's-by-the-Lake Episcopal Church, I have been able to watch JoAnn mature into the fine young lady she is today. She is a tireless worker, having given the most volunteer hours of any of our young adults in the parish. She is always cheerful and dependable.

Recommendation

I am sure that whoever hires her will find her a good worker as well as a pleasant person. She is truly a gem.

Sincerely,

Louis R. Stanley
Rector

LRS:kpw

Progress Report

An evaluation or progress report is an essential communication for anyone's career. Keep an honest, positive tone that focuses on specifics.

August 30, 199X

Chairperson
Academic Professional Development Committee
St. Paul School of Theology
5123 Truman Road
Kansas City, MO 64127

Dear Chairperson:

Purpose — Recently, the Reverend Kendall Campbell, the Registrar and Financial Aid Director at St. Paul, asked Mr. Lee Yoon Park to obtain a summary of progress for his language studies this summer. **Evaluation** — I am delighted to report to you that he is an exceptional student who would have earned an A in English had he opted for a grade and credit. **Relationship** — I was fortunate to be his instructor.

Duration of Relationship — Mr. Park spent approximately twenty-five hours of intense conversation and study of written English with me in June and July. **Character** — This time was significantly dwarfed by the vast hours of self-directed study that he completed between each of our meetings. This self-direction shows his determination to overcome any language obstacles he may still experience.

Observations — During our meetings, I was amazed at Mr. Park's insight and humor. His wit is a joy to experience and to learn from. He asks profound questions, such as, "What is your parenting philosophy?" He shares his Korean heritage and history with those of us who ask. He reads sophisticated literature — including some I have not read yet! He travels with his family and friends as often as he has the opportunity, especially making trips to national parks throughout the United States. All of these activities testify to Mr. Park's value of learning. His ability to communicate increases regularly.

Insight — Mr. Park's ability to communicate goes far beyond his knowledge of either American English or Korean — his ability touches the center of our mutual humanity. **Thank You** — Thank you for recognizing my friend's promise and for supporting his efforts.

Sincerely,

Bree Biesner, M.A.
Adjunct Faculty

Rejection of Application

The only thing worse than writing a rejection letter is receiving one. Be clear, yet gentle, in your approach.

WEST TELECOMMUNICATIONS
103 Randolph St.
Chicago, IL 60601

July 26, 199X

Janna Hazelden, Senior Actuary
Waldron Hotels
278 Main Blvd.
El Paso, TX 79902

Dear Ms. Hazelden:

Thank You

Thank you for giving us the opportunity to review your qualifications for actuary.

Rejection/Reason
Compliment
Request

Although we do not currently have an opening in our accounting department, we are always looking for competent people. May we keep your file active during the next ninety days should any possibilities open up? We will notify you immediately if a position becomes available.

Goodwill
Personal Note

In the meantime, good luck in your job search. I am sure, with your background, you will find a suitable position soon.

Sincerely,

Rod Finney
Personnel Director

Rejection of a Solicited Application

This letter is used to inform an applicant that the position for which he or she applied has been offered to someone else.

Morton Engineering
3457 Randall St. N.E. • Armond, AR 72310

January 25, 199X

K.J. Land
356 Denver
University of Nebraska
Lincoln, NE 68308

Dear Mr. Land:

Thank you for applying at Morton Engineering. I am sorry that we are unable to offer you the position of electrical engineer for which you recently interviewed.

We have selected another person who has the type of experience we feel is necessary for the position. I enjoyed interviewing you and hope that you are successful in your employment search in the near future.

If you should have any questions, please call me.

Sincerely,

Hanna Westcott
Personnel Director

HJW:kmm

Thank You
Rejection

Reason for Rejection

Goodwill

Contact Information

Rejection of an Unsolicited Application

This letter is used to inform an applicant that there are no positions available at the present time for which he or she is qualified.

First National Bank
223 Ames • Casper, WY 82676

August 30, 199X

Kelly Flanders
1795 Whisper Lane, #3
Casper, WY 82676

Dear Ms. Flanders:

Compliment / Rejection

Your qualifications are impressive. Unfortunately, we are not presently hiring bank tellers.

Reason for Rejection / Added Service

As you may know, we recently went through a major expansion. However, we have filled all of our bank teller positions and do not foresee any change in staff in the near future. We will, however, keep your application on file for one year should something arise.

Thank You

Thank you for your interest in First National. If you should have any questions, please call me.

Sincerely,

Hiram Scott
Vice President, Human Resources

HMS:ald

Invitation for an Interview

Arrange appointment specifications for easy, quick visual access. This letter can set the tone for the actual interview.

HILL MULTI-MEDIA CORPORATION
301 E. Armour Blvd. • Kansas City, MO 64111

March 5, 199X

Kay E. Anders
7923 Noland Road
Lenexa, KS 66215-2528

Dear Ms. Anders:

Thank you for your application for the position of Communications Director. We are pleased to invite you to be interviewed for the position. Your interview has been scheduled as follows: *(Acknowledgment, Request)*

Date:	March 17, 199X
Time:	11:15 a.m.
Location:	Conference Room A Second Floor (Northeast) Gillham Plaza Building 301 E. Armour Blvd. Kansas City, MO 64111
Parking:	Underground area off of Gillham Road

(Details)

You can expect to meet with the committee for 30 to 45 minutes. If you have any questions, please contact me at (816) 871-6889. *(Expectations, Contact Information)*

Again, thank you for your interest in the position. *(Thank You)*

Sincerely,

Carol J. Kennedy
Interim Director of Programs

CJK:dmc

Acknowledgment
Request

Details

Expectations
Contact Information
Thank You

Job Offer

This letter is used to offer a position to a potential employee and should be treated as a legal contract. It should outline all of the essential information the potential employee needs to make a decision.

Morton Engineering
3457 Randall St. N.E. • Armond, AR 72310

January 25, 199X

J. Wallace Mercer
7898 Talleyho Lane
Lexington, KY 40329

Dear Mr. Mercer:

Job Offer

It is with great pleasure that I am able to offer you a position at Morton Engineering as an electrical engineer.

Outline the Position

The position pays $35,000 annually in equal increments every other Friday. Additionally, you will receive two weeks' paid vacation every 12 months, a bonus equaling two weeks' salary payable the payday before Christmas, health benefits and $25,000 of life insurance. This position is a two-year agreement, after which it may be renegotiated. Either party may terminate with a two-week notice.

Welcome

We are very pleased to offer you the position and are sure that you will make a superb addition to our firm. If you have any questions, please call me at any time.

Sincerely,

Hanna Westcott
Personnel Director

HJW:kmm

Job Offer

This letter affirms the reader and the writer's choice of applicants.

Haven Home
P.O. Box 124 • Memphis, TN 38124

September 15, 199X

Kory Chandler
45 Main Drive
Memphis, TN 38118

Dear Kory:

We are pleased that your experience and education match our needs for a fundraiser and program coordinator. Your enthusiasm convinced the interview committee that you are the appropriate match for Haven Home.

Your vision for adding follow-up questionnaires to our first-time clients is a dynamic idea. That effort will initiate many improvements in our service to family members experiencing domestic violence. At the same time, the questions will increase awareness of personal choices in our clients living with violence.

The transition and training schedule for your first week at Haven Home is attached. Please review it for Monday morning at 7:30.

If there is anything I can do to help make your transition more comfortable, please let me know. My voice mail number is 64. I'll check in with you later to see how your first day is going.

Welcome to our team!

Sincerely,

Anna Phelps
Executive Director

AP:dmc

Job Offer Compliment

Contribution

Attachment

Contact Information

Welcome

New Employee

This letter welcomes a new employee to a business.

Pink's Shears, Inc.
763 Kekke Dr. — Hibbing, MN 21111

May 6, 199X

Linda Jean Tripp
1205 Mickey Mouse Dr.
Orlando, FL 32078

Dear Ms. Tripp:

First Welcome

It is my distinct pleasure to welcome you to Pink's Shears, Inc. We are looking forward to your arrival on May 21.

General Comments
Specific Position

We at Pink's are very proud of our complete line of pinking shears and know that you will take the same pride in your work as we do in ours. Your role as Sales Director will be an important one. We know that with your education and experience you will bring to Pink's a much-needed momentum.

Second Welcome

Once again, welcome to Pink's. If there is any way I can help you make the transition, let me know.

Sincerely,

Harold "Pinky" Pinkham
President

HJP:cpa

Promotion — Congratulations

This letter congratulates an employee or business associate on his promotion.

Cadrell's
290 26th Ave. • Winston, GA 30067

August 8, 199X

T. Molly Rathburn
8944 Tripp
Winston, GA 30067

Dear Molly:

I would like to congratulate you on your recent promotion to Assistant Plant Supervisor. You must be proud of your accomplishments.

Because of your hard work and dedication, you deserve this promotion. Employees like you help Cadrell's keep ahead of the competition and lead the way in the field of dental equipment. Your efforts are appreciated.

Congratulations again. Welcome to the management team at Cadrell's.

Sincerely yours,

J.K. Cadrell, Jr.
President

JKC:ltj

First Congratulations

General Statement (optional)

Second Congratulations

Announcing a Promotion — Personal

This letter announces the promotion of an employee.

Nacogdoches Notebooks
277 Linden • Nacogdoches, TX 75963

August 1, 199X

Truc Phan
3009 Clipclop Lane
Nacogdoches, TX 75963

Dear Mr. Phan:

Announcement

We are pleased to offer you the promotion to Vice-President in Charge of Sales.

Reason

Nacogdoches Notebooks is promoting you because of your outstanding and untiring commitment to your work. Nacogdoches Notebooks has grown substantially because of your efforts.

Instructions

Please see Ray Norton on Monday. He will show you your new office and begin your orientation.

Welcome

Congratulations. We are proud to have you associated with us.

Sincerely,

Susanna M. Graham
President

SMG:eer

Announcing a Promotion — Internal

This memo announces the promotion of an employee to other members of the firm. In certain circumstances a letter may be used also.

MEMORANDUM

Date: August 5, 199X
To: All Employees
From: Susanna Graham, President
Re: Promotion to Vice President/Sales

Announcement

We are pleased to announce the promotion of Truc Phan to Vice-President in Charge of Sales.

Reason

In the past 12 months, Mr. Phan has consistently provided outstanding service to his clients, brought in several new accounts and demonstrated outstanding sales leadership. Nacogdoches Notebooks has grown substantially because of Mr. Phan's work. He will assume his new position on August 10 and will be located in Suite 25.

Welcome

Please join me in congratulating Mr. Phan on his new position.

Acceptance of Resignation

Always accept resignation with dignity. Allow the letter to reflect your personal investment in the relationship. This letter shows a friendship exists. If that is not your situation, omit the personal comments.

Merl Garrett, Supervisor of Nurses
University Medical Center
5000 University Parkway
Laguna Heights, CA 92677

May 12, 199X

Sherri Lu, Senior Floor Nurse
University Medical Center
5020 University Parkway
Laguna Heights, CA 92677

Dear Sherri:

Regret / Acceptance / Reason

We regret you must leave and reluctantly accept your resignation as senior floor nurse beginning June 1, 199X. We do, however, understand that personal medical concerns demand your attention now.

Contributions / Thank You

Your contributions to University Medical Center will remain after your departure: better documentation, better patient service and improved staff morale. Thank you for your hard work in every aspect of your job. Your dedication to us shows in your willingness to help train your replacement. We have always been able to count on you.

Goodwill / Personal Note

We wish you the best health. I will miss you immensely. Please stay in touch.

Sincerely,

Merl

Checklist

- ☐ Did you use a positive tone?
- ☐ Does the letter specify the terms of employment?
- ☐ Does the letter request specific information?
- ☐ Did you summarize, thank or restate in the last part of the letter?
- ☐ If you received the letter, would you know what to do?
- ☐ Does your letter show respect for confidentiality?
- ☐ Is your letter personal?

Chapter 11 — Customer Relations Letters

Sample letters that improve or maintain good customer relations sell a company's image. The broad categories are as follows:

At the side of the page, you will find a brief explanation of each part of the letter. The first letter, on page 157, identifies each section of the letter. Subsequent letters identify only changes to the basic format.

Writing Customer Relations Letters

Step-by-Step Guide

Recent research sheds some light on the importance of maintaining good customer relations. Consider these facts:

- *96% of unhappy customers never let a business know they are unhappy.*
- *A customer will tell an average of 9 or 10 people about a bad experience, but will tell only 4 or 5 about a good one.*
- *A business will spend five times as much to acquire a new customer as it does to serve an existing one.*

— adapted from ***Customer Service: The Key to Winning Lifetime Customers*** *by Marian Thomas; published by National Press Publications*

These letters are designed to improve or maintain customer relations. The maxim that the customer is always right should be kept in mind while writing these letters. At times, however, you may have to let the customer think he is right while you are proving him wrong!

Step 1: The first part of the letter states your purpose. This may be anything from acknowledging a complaint to notifying a customer of a move.

Step 2: The second part of the letter explains the purpose. If the first part acknowledges a complaint, then the second part explains what you are going to do about it. If the first part announces a new address to valued customers, then the second part gives the details about the new location's conveniences.

Step 3: The last part is the sugar to leave a good taste in the customer's mouth. It summarizes the letter, thanks the customer and reiterates the customer's value to your organization.

Note: At the end of this chapter is a checklist to use when you write a customer relations letter.

General Appreciation

This letter is used to show appreciation for your customers. It may be used as a sales and promotional letter or a thank-you for continued patronage.

Zebra Prints **224 Bever Ave. • Madrid, MS 39378**	Letterhead
October 12, 199X	Date
Lillian R. Wilkinson 4500 Ramble Road Lane Madrid, MS 39379	Inside Address
Dear Ms. Wilkinson:	Salutation
On behalf of Zebra Prints we wish to express our sincerest appreciation for your continued patronage. It is because of valued customers like you that we are able to continue to offer you the finest in fabrics.	Statement of Purpose Compliment
Zebra Prints has been in business for 75 years. We are dedicated to bringing you the finest in fabrics, particularly those of all-natural materials. Mr. Case, our founding father, loved to say, "The customer wants the best at the lowest price," and that is the motto we use as our guiding principle.	Elaboration
Please stop in and see us soon. Our new spring fabrics will be in the showroom on March 15. If you bring this letter with you, we will give you a 15% discount on any fabric you purchase in March.	Summary Benefit
Sincerely yours,	Complimentary Close
Terrance Sullivan Case, Jr. President	Signature
TSC:maj	Additional Information

Acknowledging a Complaint

This letter is used to acknowledge a complaint and offer a solution to the problem.

Tiny Toes Dance Studio
33 Barbara Dr. • Butte, MT 59777

September 2, 199X

Mickey Wu
790 7th St.
Butte, MT 59777

Dear Mr. Wu:

Acknowledgment of Complaint

Thank you for your letter of August 30 discussing our policy concerning payment for missed classes.

Solution

I have checked with our owner, Ms. Timberlane, for a clarification. In the past our policy was that missed classes would still need to be paid for. Under the circumstances, however, she said that you will not have to pay for the classes your daughter missed because of her unfortunate accident on the way to class.

Summary

Thank You

We hope this is a satisfactory solution for you and wish your daughter, Jasmine, a speedy recovery. We shall put a hold on your account until she is ready to return to her tap lessons. Thank you once again for your concern.

Sincerely yours,

Mary Manson
Business Manager

MLM:wmj

Following Up on a Complaint

Once a complaint is logged and your company has resolved it, send a follow-up letter as an extra effort toward redeeming your reputation for good service. Here is an example.

McGiven Publishing Company
29 New York Ave.
New York City, NY 10022

May 21, 199X

Steve Laing
444 Madison St.
Livingston, NJ 07039

Dear Mr. Laing:

Our service goal is to fill your orders accurately 100% of the time, but now and then we fall short and errors occur. It's frustrating for everyone when things go wrong.

I'm sorry you had a problem with your recent order, and I hope the situation has been resolved to your satisfaction. If there is anything else we can do for you, please call us toll-free at 1-800-238-5225 Monday through Friday between 7 a.m. and 4 p.m. Eastern time.

Thanks for your patience and understanding.

Sincerely,

Peg Mahr
Customer Service Manager

PM:hs

Goal
Acknowledgment of Error

Apology
Goodwill
Assistance Offer
Contact Information

Thanks

Regaining a Customer's Confidence

"A soft answer turneth away wrath."

—Proverbs 15:1

Use this letter to smooth relations with a disgruntled customer and regain his or her confidence in your firm.

MODERN MEDICAL SUPPLIES
302 Main — Portland, OR 97272

November 23, 199X

Dr. Laura Schmitt
1520 Barston Blvd.
Sacramento, CA 95808

Dear Dr. Schmitt:

Statement of Purpose

Please accept our sincerest apologies for the recent mix-up with the shipment of tongue depressors. I can assure you that action has been taken to remedy the problem in our warehouse.

Regaining of Confidence

Result

Thank You

As a token of good faith we have deducted 15% from your bill. We hope that this will help compensate for any inconvenience this problem caused. We have dismissed our head shipping clerk because of this unfortunate incident. After checking, we discovered a number of glaring errors he had made. Thank you for bringing the error to our attention.

Summary of Order Information

We hope that this will be a satisfactory solution. Your corrected order of tongue depressors should be arriving shortly, as they were sent November 22.

Sincerely yours,

Graham Johnson
Customer Relations

GJJ:amr

Acknowledging a Complaint — Disclaiming Responsibility

This letter acknowledges a customer's complaint in order to maintain good relations; however, it refers the customer to another source that is responsible for the problem.

Peoria Pet Foods
3005 Lincolnway • Peoria, IL 61635

March 30, 199X

Mary Louise Jones
Paws R Us
8900 Waconia
Joliet, IL 60434

Dear Ms. Jones:

Thank you for bringing the problem of late deliveries to our attention. I'm sure they must be most aggravating.

As much as we would like to help you, the problem lies with the trucking firm and not here at Peoria Pet Foods. We have contacted them concerning the late deliveries and are reviewing our use of Nelson Trucking as our carrier. At present we have no contract with them, but shall be demanding a contract so that we have leverage in such matters. I suggest that you contact them, also, to emphasize the seriousness of the situation.

I'm sorry I can't help you any more than this, but I can assure you that we are trying to remedy the situation as quickly as we can. Unfortunately, an immediate solution is dependent upon Nelson Trucking. Thank you once again for your understanding.

Sincerely yours,

Lucy McAlister
Customer Relations

LJM:glu

Acknowledgment of Complaint

Disclaimer of Responsibility

Action Taken

Result

Suggestion

Apology

Thank You

Acknowledging a Complaint — Explaining a Misunderstanding

Acknowledge a customer's complaint in order to maintain good relations by explaining a misunderstanding between the customer and the business

RTM, Inc.
P.O. Box 2089 • Milwaukee, WI 53219

January 16, 199X

Thomas R. Linder
Bottlers' Distributors
7035 Wacker
Milwaukee, WI 53227

Dear Mr. Linder:

Acknowledgment of Complaint

I appreciate your bringing to my attention the problem of our Colden Beer and its introductory flyer. I understand your confusion perfectly.

Explain Misunderstanding

When we sent you the letter introducing our new beer, our marketing department mistakenly sent a mock-up of an ad for Eagle's Wings Ale. Naturally, you would be confused because we were referring to the blue eagle on Colden Beer while giving you the bald eagle label of Eagle's Wings Ale.

Apology

We are most sorry for this error and have enclosed a corrected flyer.

Thank You

I hope that this letter and the enclosed corrected flyer clear up this unfortunate misunderstanding. Thank you once again for bringing this to my attention.

Sincerely,

R. Edwards Rands
Public Relations Director

RER:kks

Correcting an Error

Correct an error that either the customer caught or that the business caught.

CAPITAL CREDIT UNION
890 Minnesota Ave. • Washington, D.C. 20041

April 24, 199X

Mr. and Mrs. John Gallup
3256 Mozart Dr.
Silver Spring, MD 20743

Dear Mr. and Mrs. Gallup:

After our current auditing we discovered an underpayment to your account of $53.23 in interest.

The error occurred in the transferring of funds in March from your High-Fi account to your regular savings account. We have corrected your savings account and credited you with $53.23.

I hope this is satisfactory, and I apologize for any confusion this error caused. Thank you for your continued patronage.

Sincerely,

Molly Butters
Vice President, Accounting

MMB:tli

Statement of Error

Explanation
Correction

Apology
Thank You

General Apology

This letter is used to apologize to customers.

MERKERS DEPARTMENT STORE
1115 Brandon — New Ulm, MN 56053

July 22, 199X

Kim Langworth
R.R. 1
Red Earth, MN 56670

Dear Ms. Langworth:

Apology

We at Merker's would like to extend our sincerest apologies and ask for your understanding.

Explanation

Decision

Benefit

Our recent sales brochure made claims that we could not follow through on. Not all merchandise in the Summer Saver Sale was on sale at 50% off. The printer inadvertently left out the important word "selected." Because of this glaring error, we have decided to postpone our sale and reschedule it for another time. By postponing the sale we will be able to offer you even better bargains than we had originally planned.

Thank You

Thank you for your understanding in this embarrassing situation.

Sincerely,

R. Merker
Chairman of the Board

RCM:hhh

Acknowledging an Order — Back Order

This letter is used to acknowledge that a customer's order has been received, but that it is back-ordered, thus causing a delay.

Todmann Nuts and Bolts
P.O. Box 3445 • Idaho Falls, ID 83406

June 3, 199X

Timothy R. Johnson, Purchasing
Sheppard Hardware Distributors
P.O. Box 1078
Kansas City, MO 64109-1078

Dear Mr. Johnson:

We are pleased to receive your order for 10,000 quarter-inch nuts, part number XK22345JM. However, we are unable at this time to fulfill that order.

Acknowledgment of Order

Our present inventory has been depleted and that nut is now on back-order until mid-July. Our supplier of raw materials is unable to supply the materials until July 1, thus pushing us back to mid-July for possible delivery. We have tried without success to find an alternate source of raw materials. If you like, we could substitute part number XK22346JM. It is a penny higher in price per unit. Otherwise, we will keep your order and rush it to you as soon as we can start production in these nuts again. Please let us know your preference this week.

Explanation

Alternative (optional)

Thank you for your understanding in this matter. We apologize for your inconvenience.

Thank You
Apology

Sincerely,

Cass Walker
Production Head

CBW:pst

Acknowledging an Order — Explaining Shipment Procedures

Explain a shipping procedure to a customer while acknowledging that an order has been received.

Raging Bull Farms
R.R. 2 • Kingman, OK 73439

August 13, 199X

Natalie Gorman
Cherokee Crafts
900 E. Main
Tulsa, OK 74102

Dear Ms. Gorman:

Acknowledgment of Order

Thank you for your order of 25 authentic Cherokee head-dresses on August 11, 199X. We will be sending those immediately.

Explanation
Action Plan
Alternative Plan

Because of the fragile nature of our head-dresses, we hand deliver to our customers within Oklahoma. Our delivery day for Tulsa is Friday, which means that your head-dresses will arrive this coming Friday, August 17. If this is unsatisfactory, please call us so that we can arrange an alternative delivery date.

Thank You

Thank you for your business. I'm sure that you will be most pleased with our head-dresses, and we look forward to working with you in the future.

Sincerely yours,

Tamara Whitewater

TJW:zmd

Apologizing for an Employee's Action

Apologize for the action of one of your employees who has damaged customer relations.

Belle's Phone Store
Windale Mall
8855 Outer Dr. • Waukegan, IL 60079

November 3, 199X

Travis C. Schultz
5554 Rocky Shore Dr.
North Waukegan, IL 60079

Dear Mr. Schultz:

I wish to personally apologize for your unfortunate treatment by our employee, Betty Robertson, last Friday. Her actions toward you were totally inappropriate.

Because of this situation, we have relieved Ms. Robertson of her position. We would also like to offer you a gift certificate for $50 of merchandise at our store. We value our customers and hope that this token will help compensate for the embarrassment you felt. We are increasing our training in customer relations for all of our employees to avoid just such a problem occurring again.

Thank you for your business and your understanding. We hope that this is a satisfactory solution to the problem.

Sincerely yours,

Belle June Maples

BJM:kio

Apology

Action Taken (optional)

Goal of Customer Satisfaction

Result

Thank You

Notifying Customers of a Move

Notify customers of a move and assure them that the move will not affect them or will be advantageous to them.

MARCO PAPER CLIPS
P.O. Box 22, Marquette, MI 49855

May 4, 199X

K.J. Wasserman
City Business Supply
763 C. St. S.W.
Columbia, MO 65205

Dear Mr. Wasserman:

Announcement

On July 1, 199X, Marco Paper Clips will be moving to Des Moines, Iowa. This move should greatly benefit your company.

Elaboration

Benefits

We are excited about the move to Des Moines. Our move will help you receive shipments more quickly. It will also reduce the cost of shipping to Marco and we can pass those savings on to you. Des Moines' larger labor market also allows us to expand our facilities and product line. We feel that this will definitely benefit our customers.

Summary

Contact Information

Please feel free to contact us if you have any concerns. Our new address in Des Moines will be: Marco Paper Clips, 3567 Grandview, Des Moines, IA 54421. Our toll-free number will be 800-BUY-CLIP.

Sincerely,

G. Antonio Marco
President

GAM:etv
Enc.

Holiday Greetings

This letter is used to send holiday greetings to your customers.

Flatt Tire Co.
223 Nueva Matica, Santa Cruz, CA 95066

December 5, 199X

Theodore "Bubba" Brown
Glendale Amoco
Highway 13
Glendale, CA 90046

Dear Mr. Brown:

Flatt Tire Co. would like to wish you and your employees the very best this holiday season. We hope that you are blessed with customers as great as you.

We are most fortunate to have customers like Glendale Amoco and hope that this coming new year we can continue our relationship. We know that our prosperity depends on our customers.

Thank you for helping make Flatt Tire Co. one of the leaders in Southern California. Our fondest regards for all of you at Glendale Amoco.

Happy Holidays,

Rhonda J. Flatt
President

RJF:alc

Greetings

Elaboration
(optional)

Thank You
Goodwill

Writing Customer Relations Letters

Checklist

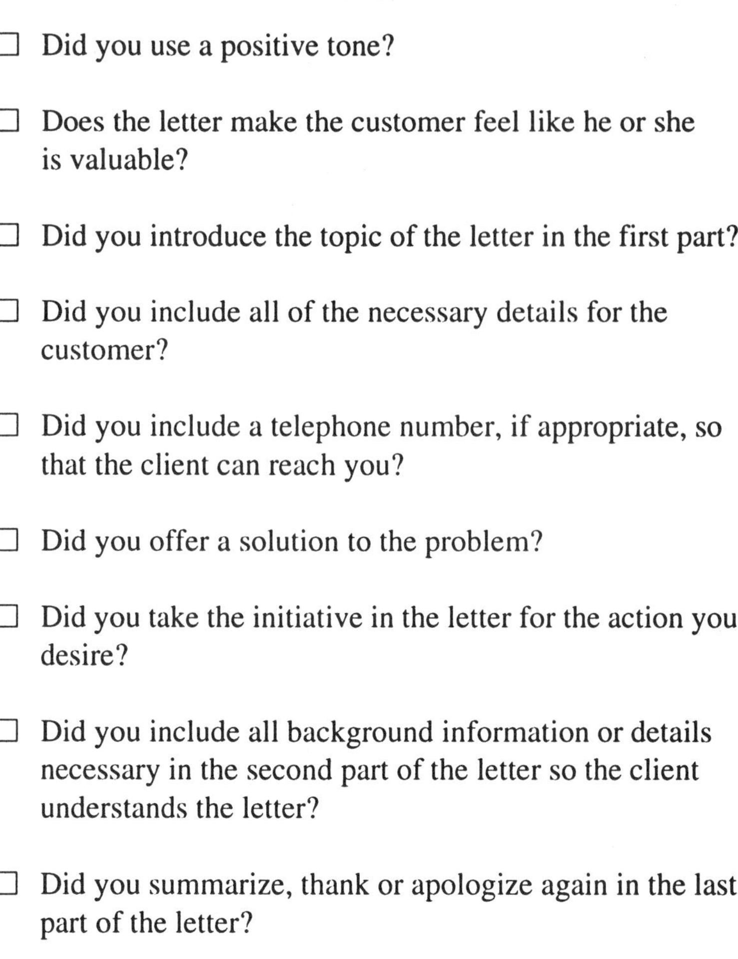

☐ Did you use a positive tone?

☐ Does the letter make the customer feel like he or she is valuable?

☐ Did you introduce the topic of the letter in the first part?

☐ Did you include all of the necessary details for the customer?

☐ Did you include a telephone number, if appropriate, so that the client can reach you?

☐ Did you offer a solution to the problem?

☐ Did you take the initiative in the letter for the action you desire?

☐ Did you include all background information or details necessary in the second part of the letter so the client understands the letter?

☐ Did you summarize, thank or apologize again in the last part of the letter?

☐ If you received the letter, how would you feel?

Chapter 12 — Media Letters

12

Here are samples to help you write letters to the media (newspapers, television stations, magazines). The broad categories are as follows:

At the side of the page, you will find a brief explanation of each part of the letter. The first letter, on page 173, identifies each section of the letter. Subsequent letters identify only changes to the basic format.

Writing Media Letters

Step-by-Step Guide

Media letters are used in business as a way to get the public's attention. Media exposure is free advertising and the smart business person uses it to sell his business and its services or products. The letter in and of itself is a sales tool.

Step 1: The first part of the letter or press release states your purpose. This may be anything from announcing a new employee to responding to an editorial.

Step 2: The second part of the letter or press release explains the first part by giving details and examples about the first part. This part should include all pertinent information concerning the event or situation. If, for example, you are announcing a new employee, you would in the second part give the details about the employee. Always answer the questions Who? What? When? Where? Why? and if appropriate, How? in this section.

Step 3: The last part of the letter acts as a summary reminding the recipient of the general nature of the letter. It may also be used as a thank-you.

Note: At the end of this chapter is a checklist to use when you write a media letter.

Media Event Letter — Sales Campaign Kickoff

Alert the media to a sales campaign kickoff and invite the media to cover the event.

Capital Crystal **449 Worthington • Charleston, WV 25009**	Letterhead
March 16, 199X	Date
Todd Phillips, Station Manager KOAL 2525 Kanawah Charleston, WV 25009	Inside Address
Dear Mr. Phillips:	Salutation
On March 25, Capital Crystal will announce the winner of our "How Many Goblets in a Dump Truck" contest. We will do so at noon in front of our business at 449 Worthington.	Announcement
Our "How Many Goblets in a Dump Truck" contest has been going on now for approximately three months and one of the more than 4,000 entrants will be the lucky winner of $1,000. We will also donate $1,000 to Charleston's Homeless Shelter at that time. With the announcement we will dump the goblets out of the truck and onto the ground. Wade Wilson and His Debonnaires will play during the reception that follows.	Explanation Specific Details
We are sure that this event would be of interest to your viewers of "Eye on Charleston" at noon because of the huge response we have had to the contest. Thank you for your interest.	Summary Thank You
Sincerely yours,	Complimentary Close
Candice Trotter President	Signature
CJT:lsj	Additional Information

Media Event Letter — Recently Published Book

Notify the media of a recently published book.

DONALDSON'S
223 Niagara Dr. • Buffalo, NY 14290

September 12, 199X

Mary Beth Parkinson
WWJ
874 7th St.
Buffalo, NY 14292

Dear Ms. Parkinson:

Announcement

I have recently published a book called *Entrepreneur at Risk.* I am sending you a copy to review.

Explanation

Persuasion

The topic is worthy of your morning show, "Good Morning Buffalo," and I would be interested in discussing the book as a guest on your show. The premise is that entrepreneurs are at risk in the U.S. and will soon be an endangered species. This is a very timely topic with an upcoming forum on entrepreneurs at the Carmine Colosseum.

Summary

Thank You

I have enclosed my biographical sketch, a synopsis of the book and a press release from my publishing house. I hope that you will have time to look at these. Thank you for your attention.

Sincerely,

Larry J. Beiers
President

LJB:wuy

Media Event Letter — Anniversary

Use this letter to alert the media of your company's anniversary.

Evanson Buick
7793 Sahara Way • Reno, NV 89585

May 19, 199X

Wayne Wilson
KBET
444 Plaza Dr.
Reno, NV 89588

Dear Mr. Wilson:

On May 29 Evanson Buick will be 50 years old, making us the oldest car dealership in Nevada. We will be staging a three-day celebration.

On May 29, we will kick off our anniversary with free hot air balloon rides and an ascension at 6 p.m. On May 30, we will have the oldest race car driver, Judd MacElroy, signing autographs from 2 to 4 p.m. On May 31, we will have our drawing for a Buick Reatta at 5:30 p.m. followed by a picnic open to the public. During all three days there will be displays of antique autos and carnival rides for the children. We think that our anniversary event would make a fine spot on your "Neighbors" segment on the 6 o'clock news.

I have enclosed a flyer describing the complete festivities. Thank you for helping us celebrate our anniversary.

Sincerely,

M. Art Evanson
President

MAE:fsw
Enc.

Announcement

Explanation

Specific Details

Summary
Thank You

Press Release — Anniversary

Use this press release to alert the media in general of a company's anniversary.

Darling's Cookies
309 Watertown Road • Tacoma, WA 98438

January 29, 199X
FOR IMMEDIATE RELEASE

Announcement

On February 5, 199X, Darling's Cookies will celebrate its 50th anniversary, making us the oldest bakery in Tacoma and the second oldest in the Tri-State area.

Explanation
Specific Details

Darling's Cookies was established on February 5, 1940, by Darrel Darling. At first, Darling's employed only three people and was located on Front Street in downtown Tacoma. After the war, Darling's moved to its present location on Watertown Road and now employs 25 people full-time. Darling's specialties are cinnamon rolls, chocolate chip cookies and its patented double chocolate fudge bar. Darling's will host an open house on February 5 at its plant. We are expecting children from several local schools, residents from several nursing homes and group houses, as well as our regular patrons. Please stop by for free refreshments.

Contact
Information

FOR MORE INFORMATION CONTACT:
Darrel Darling, Jr.
President
627-2211

Press Release — Speaking Engagement

Use this press release to alert the media of an upcoming speech.

Los Gatos Community College
2312 College Dr. • Los Gatos, NM 87531
505-829-6636

April 2, 199X
FOR IMMEDIATE RELEASE

Dr. Larry Thompson, noted historian, will speak April 20, 199X, at Los Gatos Community College. He will speak on "History in the Making: How Current Events Redefine Our Lives."

Dr. Thompson is a leading authority on trends in history. He is professor of history from Cornell University in Ithaca, NY. He is presently on leave from the university so that he can lecture around the world on this topic. His speech has been well received throughout the United States. He will explain how the fall of the Berlin Wall has affected all of us. After the speech Dr. Thompson will hold a symposium on American business trends. He will autograph copies of his best seller, *Wake Up America*, in the lobby of the Emerson Auditorium prior to his speech at 7 p.m.

FOR MORE INFORMATION CONTACT:
Sara Thompson
Public Relations Department
Los Gatos Community College

Announcement
Topic

Explanation

Specific Details

Contact Information

Press Release — Promotion

Use this press release to notify the media of a promotion within your business.

OGDEN MANUFACTURING
58 Brigham Young Dr. • Ogden, UT 84404
801-782-9889

August 30, 199X
FOR IMMEDIATE RELEASE

Announcement

Ogden Manufacturing announces the promotion of Paul K. Van Daan to Vice President, Accounting. He will replace Terrance Reilly, who is retiring.

Explanation

Specific Details

Paul Van Daan joined Ogden Manufacturing in March 19XX, as an accountant and was promoted in 19XX to Department Head, Accounts Receivable. In 19XX he was promoted to Division Head, Customer Relations. He is a graduate of Brigham Young University and is a Certified Public Accountant. Previously, he worked for Dowling Box, Ltd.

Contact Information

FOR MORE INFORMATION CONTACT:
David Conrad
Human Resources Office
Ogden Manufacturing

A black and white photo is enclosed.

Press Release — New Employee

Use this press release to announce to the media that a new employee will be joining your firm.

KLINGER BLINDS
2221 Washington • Flagstaff, AZ 86093

October 17, 199X
FOR IMMEDIATE RELEASE

Klinger Blinds announces that Karen M. Bark has been hired as our Director of Sales. She will start in her new position on November 1.

Karen M. Bark is a native of Southern California and has previously been employed by Tremore Window Treatments in Los Angeles as Sales Coordinator. She has a degree in Interior Design from the Design Institute in San Francisco. Ms. Bark's design for Home Lovely's "Home Beautification Project" won first place last year in the prestigious competition.

FOR MORE INFORMATION CONTACT:
Trish Klinger
Klinger Blinds

A black and white photo is enclosed.

Announcement

Explanation

Specific Details

Contact Information

Response to Editorial — Positive

Use this letter to respond to an editorial when your firm agrees.

GREATER AUGUSTA MERCHANTS
651 Main • Augusta, ME 04326

September 22, 199X

Bonnie Ervin, Station Director
WKLT Radio
1500 Walker
Augusta, ME 04325

Dear Ms. Ervin:

Announcement

We, the Greater Augusta Merchants, wish to commend you for the stand you have taken against parking meters in downtown Augusta. Your editorial of September 20 was well thought out.

Explanation

Specific Details

We feel that placing parking meters in downtown Augusta will discourage our customers from coming downtown to shop. Your report of other nearby cities who have recently installed parking meters and have seen a drop in customers demonstrates that parking meters could create the same problem if the city government passes this ordinance. We strongly urge you to continue to speak out against this issue.

Thank You

Thank you for your support for our position.

Sincerely,

Marvin Quackenbush
Executive Secretary

MJQ:omr

Response to Editorial — Negative

Use this letter to respond to an editorial when your firm disagrees.

Greater Augusta Merchants
651 Main • Augusta, ME 04326

October 20, 199X

Bonnie Ervin, Station Director
WKLT Radio
1500 Walker
Augusta, ME 04325

Dear Ms. Ervin:

Although we agree with your previous editorials opposing parking meters in downtown Augusta, we are not in agreement with your editorial of September 20. We can see no value in turning the downtown business district into a mall-like area.

To resurface our streets and make them into malls will irreversibly damage businesses downtown. The city engineers estimate the mall project will disrupt business for a minimum of a full year. Many downtown businesses are now struggling to stay alive and the mall project would be their death knell. Additionally, when completed, we would have 50% fewer parking places for our customers. Perhaps the downtown area does need cosmetic surgery, but not when it devastates the area's economy.

Thank you for your understanding of our opposition. We hope that you will reconsider your position.

Sincerely,

Marvin Quackenbush
Executive Secretary

MJQ:omr

Announcement

Explanation

Specific Details

Concession
Persuasion

Thank You

Letter Asking to Make a Speech

Use this letter when you want to make a speech or presentation.

J.P. Gaslight and Co.
790 Eastern Ave. • Ithaca, NY 14743

May 7, 199X

Calvin S. Snyder, Program Chairman
Environmental Institute
445 J. Ave., East
Lincoln, NE 68302

Dear Mr. Snyder:

Request I would like to be put on the program of the upcoming Environmental Institute Workshop in October 199X, in Chicago. My presentation on acid rain and its effect on the northeastern United States fits in with your theme, "Environmental Consequences."

Explanation I have enclosed an outline of my proposed presentation. As you can see, my recent research for our firm shows the irreversible damage done to the northeastern United States by acid rain. The presentation **Specific Details** I have outlined has been well received at the Global Earth Conference in Boston and last week at the Toronto Conference for Environ- **Enclosures** mental Concerns. I have also enclosed a list of other presentations I have given on environmental issues.

Thank You Thank you for your prompt consideration.

Sincerely,

Ted Whiteman
TKW:cap

Enc.

Letter Asking for a Correction

Use this letter to request that a correction be made from a published or broadcast report.

WILLIAMS AND SONS
1002 Elm St. • Topeka, KS 66404

August 11, 199X

Arthur Church, Managing Editor
Topeka Times
333 Main
Topeka, KS 66402

Dear Mr. Church:

Your article about Williams and Sons in last Sunday's *Times* was most appreciated. However, there is one correction that needs to be made. — **Correction**

In the article you stated that Williams and Sons has grown 15% in the last year. In reality we have grown 25% in the last year, 15% of that being in the last month. Perhaps this seems like a trivial matter, but the smaller number is negative publicity for Williams. Would you please make a correction in your upcoming business news section this Sunday? — **Explanation** / **Specific Details** / **Request**

Thank you for your prompt consideration. We appreciate the fine job you have been doing. — **Thank You** / **Goodwill**

Sincerely,

C. Blake Williams
President

CBW:nbc

Writing Media Letters

Checklist

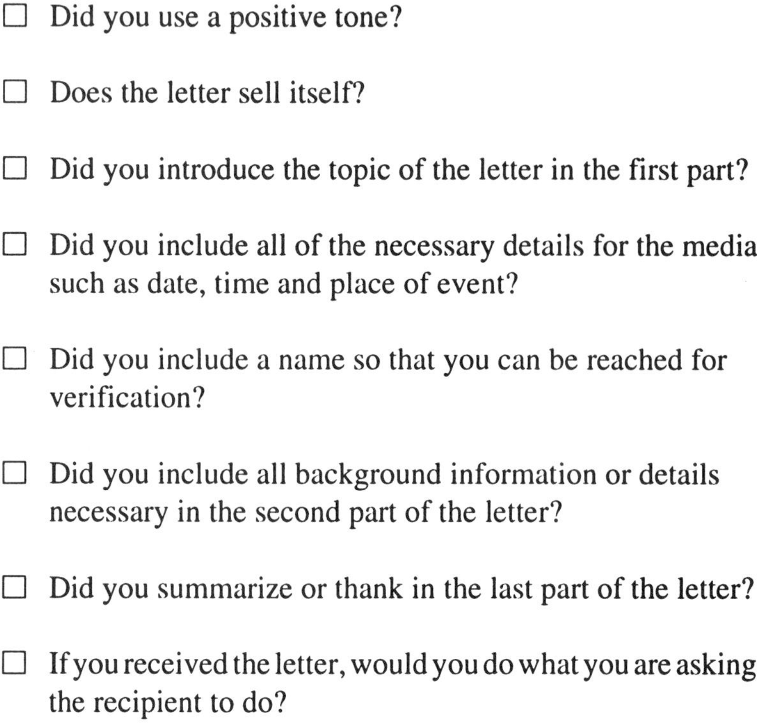

- ☐ Did you use a positive tone?
- ☐ Does the letter sell itself?
- ☐ Did you introduce the topic of the letter in the first part?
- ☐ Did you include all of the necessary details for the media such as date, time and place of event?
- ☐ Did you include a name so that you can be reached for verification?
- ☐ Did you include all background information or details necessary in the second part of the letter?
- ☐ Did you summarize or thank in the last part of the letter?
- ☐ If you received the letter, would you do what you are asking the recipient to do?

Appendix — Forms of Address

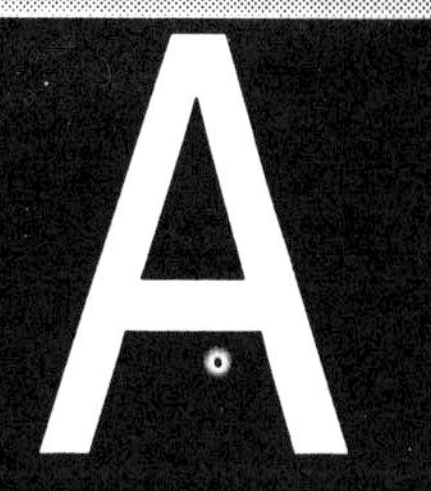

Each example lists the following information in the format shown:

Addressee
Form of Address
Salutation

The eight broad categories of address are:

- Professional Ranks and Titles
- Federal, State and Local Government Officials
- Military Ranks
- Military Abbreviations
- Diplomats
- British Nobility
- Clerical and Religious Orders
- College and University Officials

Professional Ranks and Titles

Attorney
Mr. R. Allan Whiteman, Attorney-at-Law
or R. Allan Whiteman, Esq.
Dear Mr. Whiteman:
or Dear R. Allan Whiteman, Esq.:

Dentist
Jacqueline Lyster, D.D.S.
(Office Address) or
Dr. Jacqueline Lyster
(Home Address)
Dear Dr. Lyster:

Physician

Terry Thomlinson, M.D.
(Office Address) or
Dr. Terry Thomlinson
(Home Address)
Dear Dr. Thomlinson:

Veterinarian

Cathy Hines, D.V.M.
(Office Address) or
Dr. Cathy Hines
Dear Dr. Hines:

Federal, State and Local Government Officials

Alderman

The Honorable Harriett Monson
Dear Ms. Monson:

Assemblyman

See Representative, State

Associate Justice, Supreme Court

Mr. Justice Riley
The Supreme Court of the United States
Dear Mr. Justice:

Cabinet Officers:

Secretary of State

The Honorable Emily Williamson
The Secretary of State
Dear Madam Secretary:

Attorney General

The Honorable Martin Trymore
Attorney General of the United States
Dear Sir:

Chief Justice, Supreme Court
The Chief Justice of the United States
Dear Mr. Chief Justice:

Commissioner
The Honorable C. Thomas Black
Dear Mr. Black:

Former U.S. President
The Honorable Wilson Edwards
Dear Mr. Edwards:

Governor
The Honorable Mary Simpson
Governor of Utah
Dear Governor Simpson:

Judge, Federal
The Honorable Tomas Gonzales
United States District Judge
Dear Judge Gonzales:

Judge, State or Local
Chief Judge of the Court of Appeals
The Honorable Larry Nelson
Dear Judge Nelson:

Lieutenant Governor
The Honorable Aaron Gudenkauf
Lieutenant Governor of New Jersey
Dear Mr. Gudenkauf:

Mayor
The Honorable W.M. Tied
Mayor of Greenville
Dear Mayor Tied:

Appendix — Forms of Address

President, U.S.
The President
Dear Mr. President:

Representative, State (same format for assemblyman)
The Honorable Amanda Brown
House of Representatives
State Capitol
Dear Ms. Brown:

Representative, U.S.
The Honorable Blake Grahame
The United States House of Representatives
Dear Mr. Grahame:

Senator, State
The Honorable Matthew K. Billings
The State Senate
State Capitol
Dear Senator Billings:

Senator, U.S.
The Honorable Lillian Vries
United States Senate
Dear Senator Vries:

Speaker, U.S. House of Representatives
The Honorable James B. Castle
Speaker of the House of Representatives
Dear Mr. Speaker:

Vice-President, U.S.
The Vice President
Executive Office Building
Dear Mr. Vice President

Military Ranks

Admiral, Vice Admiral, Rear Admiral

(Full Rank + Full Name + Comma + Abbreviation of Branch of Service)

Dear Admiral Rhodes:

Airman

(Full Rank + Full Name + Comma + Abbreviation of Branch of Service)

Dear Airman Smith:

Cadet

Cadet Jack Roberts
United States Military Academy

Dear Cadet Roberts:

Captain
(Air Force, Army, Coast Guard, Marine Corps or Navy)

(Full Rank + Full Name + Comma + Abbreviation of Branch of Service)

Dear Captain Lane:

Colonel, Lieutenant Colonel
(Air Force, Army or Marine Corps)

(Full Rank + Full Name + Comma + Abbreviation of Branch of Service)

Dear Colonel Arnold:

Commander
(Coast Guard or Navy)

(Full Rank + Full Name + Comma + Abbreviation of Branch of Service)

Dear Commander Grove:

Corporal

(Full Rank + Full Name + Comma + Abbreviation of Branch of Service)

Dear Corporal Jones:

First Lieutenant, Second Lieutenant (Air Force, Army or Marine Corps)

(Full Rank + Full Name + Comma + Abbreviation of Branch of Service)

Dear Lieutenant O'Shannon:

General, Lieutenant General, Major General, Brigadier General (Air Force, Army or Marine Corps)

(Full Rank + Full Name + Comma + Abbreviation of Branch of Service)

Dear General Tubbs:

Lieutenant Commander, Lieutenant, Lieutenant (JG), Ensign (Coast Guard, Navy)

(Full Rank + Full Name + Comma + Abbreviation of Branch of Service)

Dear Lieutenant Crites:

Major (Air Force, Army or Marine Corps)

(Full Rank + Full Name + Comma + Abbreviation of Branch of Service)

Dear Major Giles:

Master Sergeant (an example of other enlisted ranks having compound titles not shown here)

(Full Rank + Full Name + Comma + Abbreviation of Branch of Service)

Dear Sergeant Kaye:

Midshipman

Midshipman Sally Cole
United States Naval Academy
Dear Midshipman Cole:

Petty Officer and Chief Petty Officer Ranks

(Full Rank + Full Name + Comma + Abbreviation of Branch of Service)
Dear Mr. Schmidt:
Dear Mr. Trank: or
Dear Chief Trank:

Private

(Full Rank + Full Name + Comma + Abbreviation of Branch of Service)
Dear Private Hesse:

Seaman

(Full Rank + Full Name + Comma + Abbreviation of Branch of Service)
Dear Seaman Waters:

Specialist

(Full Rank + Full Name + Comma + Abbreviation of Branch of Service)
Dear Mr. Ledford:
Dear Ms. Fetters:

Other Ranks Not Listed

(Full Rank + Full Name + Comma + Abbreviation of Branch of Service)

Military Abbreviations

Army .... U.S.A.
Air Force .... U.S.A.F.
Marine .... U.S.M.C.
Navy .... U.S.N.

Diplomats

Ambassador to the U.S.
His Excellency Reginald Butters
The Ambassador of Bermuda
Excellency: or
Dear Mr. Ambassador:

American Ambassador
The Honorable J. Ellen Standford
Ambassador of the United States
Dear Mr. Ambassador: or
Dear Madam Ambassador:

American Charge d'Affaires
Allen White, Esq.
American Charge d'Affaires
Dear Sir:

Minister to the U.S.
The Honorable Harry Lindermann
Minister of Liechtenstein
Dear Mr. Minister:

Secretary-General, U.N.
Her Excellency Nbutu Montabi
Secretary-General of the United Nations
Dear Madam Secretary-General:

British Nobility

Baron

The Right Honorable Lord Swarthmore

Dear Lord Swarthmore: or

My Lord Swarthmore:

Baroness

The Right Honorable Lady Swarthmore

Dear Lady Swarthmore: or

My Lady Swarthmore:

Duke

His Grace, The Duke of Marlington

Dear Duke of Marlington: or

My Lord Duke:

Duchess

Her Grace, The Duchess of Marlington

Dear Duchess: or

My Lord Madam:

Duke's Younger Son

The Lord William Wymore

Dear Lord William:

Wife of Duke's Younger Son

The Lady William Wymore

Dear Lady William:

Duke's Daughter

The Lady Regina Wymore

Dear Lady Regina:

Earl
The Right Honorable the Earl of Tropingham
Dear Lord Cresswell: or
My Lord Cresswell:

Earl's Wife
The Right Honorable the Countess of Tropingham
Dear Lady Cresswell: or
Madam Cresswell:

Knight
Sir Reginald Williams
Dear Sir: or
Dear Sir Reginald:

Marquess
The Most Honorable the Marquess of Cullertshire
Dear Lord Ranson: or
My Lord Ranson:

Marchioness
The Most Honorable the Marchioness of Cullertshire
Dear Lady Ranson: or
My Lady Ranson:

Viscount
The Right Honorable the Viscount Lindsay
Dear Lord Lindsay: or
My Lord Lindsay:

Viscountess
The Right Honorable the Viscountess Lindsay
Dear Lady Lindsay: or
My Lady Lindsay:

Clerical and Religious Orders

Abbot
The Right Reverend Walter Jones, O.S.B.
Right Reverend and Abbot of St. Benedicts
Dear Father:

Archbishop
The Most Reverend Archbishop Terrance Smith
Archbishop of Canada
Your Excellency: or
Dear Archbishop:

Archbishop, Anglican
To His Grace the Lord Archbishop of Canterbury
Your Grace: or
My Dear Archbishop:

Archdeacon
The Venerable the Archdeacon of New York
Venerable Sir:

Bishop, Catholic
The Most Reverend Andrew Duncan
Bishop of New York
Your Excellency: or
Dear Bishop Duncan:

Bishop, Episcopal
The Right Reverend Samuel Thomas
Bishop of South Carolina
Dear Bishop Thomas:

Bishop, Other Denominations
The Reverend Sandra Wright
Reverend Madam: or
Dear Bishop Wright:

Brotherhood, Catholic, Member of
Brother Williams, S.J.
Dear Brother James:

Brotherhood, Catholic, Superior of
Brother Edward, S.J., Superior
Dear Brother Edward:

Canon
The Reverend Dwight Boyd
Dear Canon Boyd:

Cardinal
His Eminence, Harold Cardinal Lyte
Your Eminence: or
Dear Cardinal Lyte:

Clergyman, Protestant
The Reverend Catherine Wilson
Dear Madam: or
Dear Ms. Wilson:
(or, if having a doctor's degree)
The Reverend Dr. John Wong
Dear Dr. Wong:

Dean (of a Cathedral)
The Very Reverend Calvin Schmidt
Very Reverend Sir:
Dean Calvin Schmidt
Dear Dean Schmidt:

Monsignor
The Right Reverend Monsignor Ellis
Dear Monsignor Ellis: or
Right Reverend Monsignor

Patriarch (of an Eastern Church)
His Beatitude the Patriarch of New York
Most Reverend Lord:

Pope

His Holiness, Pope John Paul II or
His Holiness, the Pope
Your Holiness: or
Most Holy Father:

Priest, Roman Catholic

The Reverend Lynn Martin
Dear Father Martin: or
Reverend Father:

Priest, Episcopal or Anglican

The Reverend Edward Arnold
Dear Mr. Arnold: or
Dear Father Arnold:

Priest, Denominational Protestant

The Reverend Cheryl Tims
Dear Ms. Tims:

Rabbi

Rabbi Eli Gossman
Dear Rabbi Gossman:
(if having a doctor's degree)
Rabbi David Weiss, D.D.
Dear Dr. Weiss:

Sisterhood, Member of

Sister Mary Theresa, S.C.
Dear Sister Mary Theresa: or
Dear Sister:

Sisterhood, Superior of

The Reverend Mother Superior, S.C.
Reverend Mother:

College and University Officials

Dean of a College or University
Dean Mary Carlson
Dear Dean Carlson:

President of a College or University
President James Bagg
Dear President Bagg:

Professor of a College or University
Professor Linda Tripp
Dear Professor Tripp:

Note: The college official's degrees, if known, may be added after the name.

Index

A

Index

B

C

Index

E

Index

Index

R

S

Index

T

U

W